Outsider

Tales from the Road, the Trail and the Run

Proactiveoutside Publications Tulsa, Oklahoma

Cover design by Paige Benton

For Mike, who always seemed to know the way.

TABLE OF CONTENTS

PREFACE

Most stories about the outdoors have one of two winning formulas. The first is that the writer – or the subject – is someone whose exploits illicit wonder or inspiration. Their tales depict actions so fantastic that we have trouble comprehending how they did it, or what sort of person it takes to accomplish such feats.

The second normally involves a specific incident – usually something adventurous, harrowing or even tragic – that makes for a compelling story. It doesn't have to involve a famous person. The circumstances themselves are the stars of the show.

That's why folks are drawn to stories about people like Alex Honnold or Ed Viesturs, the former being the world's preeminent free-solo rock climber, and the latter being one of the greatest high-altitude mountaineers to have ever lived. It's also why stories like *Into Thin Air* have captured readers' attention for years now: The telling of the 1996 Mount Everest climbing disaster in exhaustive detail is nothing short of riveting, the high drama matched by the intense tragedy that unfolded on the upper reaches of the world's highest mountain.

These stories and many like them inspire people to explore. In some fashion we all want a story of our own.

But most of us – almost all of us, for that matter – aren't Alex Honnold, Ed Viesturs or any number of heroic daredevils and adventurers. Most of us never will be.

That doesn't mean you can't have a story of your own. Better yet, you don't have to die, get maimed, or do something audacious. You do, however, have to do *something*.

I spent a good chunk of my life doing the expected things. Sometimes the expected things are enough. But I eventually reached a point where the expected *wasn't* enough. My world was small and getting smaller as every day's wins and losses were inexorably leading me twenty-four hours closer to death. That's not the story I wanted.

Around that time I looked for things that inspired me. Some of them had roots in my childhood, others were completely new. I knew that life would have its ups and downs, but the one thing I wanted to see was a new thread woven into all of it. I'd do the hard things. I'd go places I'd never been. I'd challenge myself physically, mentally and emotionally while also having to do the expected things (the rent doesn't pay itself, you know).

Years later, I can tell you a few things. First, I'll never be a sponsored athlete or adventurer. Honnold and Viesturs have nothing to fear from me, and I'm pretty sure I'll never qualify for the Boston Marathon, or win any foot race of note.

Second, I'm glad to report that I have yet to be the subject of a sad news report. I've done some dumb things and had a few close scrapes, but at least I haven't become the tragic muse for Jon Krakauer's pen. Not yet, anyway.

But third – and most importantly – I found stories to tell that had nothing to do with my job, a game of pick-up basketball or some outrage that happened to me while driving to work. Instead, I found stories from high mountain summits and on the final stretches of a twenty-mile run. I felt what it was like to be miles deep, all alone, in a quiet, cold wilderness. Other times, I experienced things with people who possess some fantastic tales of their own.

All of this came my way without needing corporate backers, a hefty trust fund or a bit of luck in the lottery. I didn't have to sell all my stuff and live out of a van (though the thought is tempting). Like most of you, I have to work to eat and stay sheltered.

I've often told people that if I can run a marathon, so can nearly anyone else. And that's the point here. I'm no different than you. In between all those shifts at work and other daily duties, I found some stories. What follows are some of them.

This is an ongoing journey and I'm not sure where it's taking me. But I can say I am glad to have made an intentional choice to do something besides the expected. It's made the good times that much sweeter, the bad times easier to endure, and provided perspective for it all. And best yet, this isn't unique to me. Anyone can go out there and find a story of their own.

ONE: A REMINDER

"I am losing precious days. I am degenerating into a machine for making money. I am learning nothing in this trivial world of men. I must break away and get out into the mountains to learn the news."

– John Muir

Fifty feet. For all the posturing, posing and conjuring of outdoor exploits past, it had come down to this. I could only walk fifty feet before I had to stop, find some shade, sit and catch my breath. And in so doing, force the group to stop and wait on me.

The day had not gone as expected. Yes, it was hot, and the rugged terrain would test most people, but my struggle was deeper, almost comical, especially considering the lack of struggle among everyone else.

Never before had I been hiking where I felt like this. In terms of miles, we weren't all that far from a van at the trailhead, but it might as well have been on the other side of the country at the rate I was progressing, and yet there was no choice, no other avenue forward but to keep walking.

So I stood up and let the light-headedness do its thing before my equilibrium returned, waving off the heat radiating off the rocks looming overhead. I grabbed my pack – it felt heavier now than it did a few hours ago – and shrugged straps onto my shoulders, trudging ahead for another fifty feet. And then I stopped again, with a couple of questions repeatedly ringing inside my head.

What's wrong with me? How did it come to this?

****

Even a lousy day outside beats being stuck indoors. So the saying goes among the outdoorsy types.

For the most part, I think that's true. Obviously, there are exceptions: Deadly heat, a raging snowstorm, or whatever weather-induced cataclysm that might befall you. Aside from those I'll take sweltering or freezing, so long as I get to be outside somewhere interesting.

I get funny looks sometimes when I'm out for a run in the middle of winter. It might not be that cold, but cold enough for people to question my choice of attire – shorts and a light top when it's thirty degrees, for example. The same goes for summer. I won't say that pounding the trails for a couple of hours in hundred-degree heat is actually fun, but it is something that gets me outdoors, in the trees and breathing something other than recycled air.

So when people ask me why I go out there, and why not stay inside and bust off a few miles on the treadmill, my answer is the same: If the tradeoff for climate control is staring at a TV, a stats monitor, or a blank wall, I'd rather take what the outside air is offering, even if the conditions are a bit harsh.

I owe this line of thinking to a couple of things. First, I'm a bit of an escapist. I deal with everyday life OK, but there are times when I need some quiet, or a new perspective, or something different to reset my head. I've found a healthy run, a long hike or even something more ambitious, like a backpacking trip, does the trick.

Second, it's something that is ingrained in me, going way back to when I was a kid.

I was blessed to grow up in Colorado, and doubly so when my parents saved up a little money and plunked down about ten grand on a small A-frame cabin near a little burg called Bailey. The cabin itself sat on an acre-and-a-half of pine forest, accessible only by a narrow, twisty dirt road that our family's massive '69 Chevy Caprice could barely navigate.

The cabin itself was somewhat spare, but perfect just the same. We had to haul in our own water, and the toilet was outside, a two-holer outhouse. But the cabin had electricity, was fully furnished, and sported a sweet deck with a hummingbird feeder that entertained me endlessly.

The cabin served as base camp for a lot of outdoor adventures, usually short hikes into the woods looking for places to build a fort and play Army with my brothers and the friends they brought with them. On one such hike, we went pretty far from the cabin (or so it seemed through my six-year-old eyes), then stumbled into a sunlit grotto of pines and aspens. Beams of light pierced through the leaves and pine boughs, illuminating this little corner of the forest in an array of green hues that stopped me in my tracks.

I don't know how the rest of the gang reacted when they saw it, but it was a real Lady of the Lake moment for me (minus the water, of course), like I was Arthur looking for Excalibur, and there it was, being thrust from the brush by the arm of some previously unseen wood nymph. If you want to know where my sense of wonder with the outdoors came from, it was there, in that spot, on that day.

Back at the cabin, my mom whipped up dinner that cannot be adequately described in words of praise. She's that good. Our bellies full, we relaxed to mid-'70s tunes oozing from the 1930s-era wooden console radio that came with the cabin and watched the sky transform from blue to various shades of yellow, orange, red and purple. No sense of contentment was higher as we played games, pieced together puzzles or read a book.

Fishing was the other activity that got me outdoors. For a short stint, I lived in a small, northern Illinois town called Marengo, located not far from the Wisconsin border. My oldest brother Mike would often take me to the Kishwaukee River to fish for northern pike – he ended up catching a few of those, while all I ever snagged were carp. But I had better luck on the farm ponds, reeling in bluegill and other sunfish while also hooking some bass.

I can still recall the exact moment I caught my first big bass. It was at a friend's pond on a hot summer day, and I was casting just beyond some sunfish nesting grounds when I felt a tug on the line, then saw a green flash turn in the water as a decent-sized lunker sucked in my lure. It fought a good, hard fight for the better part of a minute before I pulled it from the water. I was a proud little dude that day.

After that, I spent copious amounts of cash on lures and fishing magazines, reading about anglers trying their luck in the most exotic places in the world – the Orinoco River in Venezuela, or high in the Canadian Rockies of Alberta and British Columbia, to name a few. Most kids my age were into comic books, with fantasies of flying through the skies like Superman. I dreamed of finding virgin streams in the Alaska backcountry, on the prowl for trophy salmon half as big as me.

We moved back to Colorado shortly after that, and I found another willing partner in my brother-in-law, Mark. A native Texan, he'd long taken to the outdoors, either fishing or hunting, and Colorado proved to be quite the playground. He showed me the ropes of fishing trout streams, and in short order I got pretty good at reading the waters and filling stringers with pan-worthy rainbows, brookies and browns.

On those Illinois farm ponds, the star attractions were always the fish. The Rockies were a different story. Coming from Denver and heading west, we'd drive through the foothills and the Front Range, then weave our way southwest toward Buena Vista, and just as we rounded a corner, there they were – the mighty Collegiate Peaks of the Sawatch Range, the big beasts of the Colorado Rockies erupting from the valley floor. In my mind, the only thought was "whoaaa…."

The next morning, we broke camp at a spot near a little village called Tincup and scoured the streams for beaver ponds. We lit those ponds up, catching more fish than we could legally take home, but again, that's not the image that stuck. Instead, it was the clear waters themselves, fed from the winter's snowpack, revealing blood-red rocks that constituted the riverbed at my feet. Those pristine streams, and the high peaks of the Sawatch all around, kept me going back for years.

All through junior high and high school, and well into college, I would fish, hunt, hike, ski or paddle – any sort of activity that you can imagine – just to break away from the 'burbs. I did the video game thing for a couple of years in junior high, but I can't remember any high score or electronic adventure that left an imprint quite like those rivers in the Rockies.

If I could have found a way to make a living fishing for trout, trust me, I would have done it. Nothing would have pleased me more than to carry the outdoor passions of my youth into adulthood and never look back. Peter Pan was on to something, in my estimation.

Others I knew had, at least in their own ways. A high school friend of mine named Tod headed to the mountains and did the ski bum thing for a while, working at a resort as an instructor while spending his off time getting a few turns of his own. In the slow times, he worked in local shops, making a few bucks to fund the mountain lifestyle that he and so many others loved.

I don't know how much money he made, but my guess is that it wasn't much. Folks in that world often go through lean times in the "shoulder" seasons, those months when it's too cold for rafting but not snowy enough for skiing. The outdoor life has its charms, but prosperity isn't one of them. Tod eventually gave that up, took a job with his father's company and now runs it. Tod doesn't worry about money in the shoulder seasons anymore.

My detour toward a career started right after college. I had to grow up, get a job, and build a life. That's what young adults are expected to do, and for good reason – at some point, you have to pay your own bills, write rent checks and eat. When I started out at six bucks an hour writing sports stories for a small daily newspaper, I had nowhere to go but up.

Not surprisingly, building a career took time. When you're an unproven twenty-something, you have to pay your dues, and that means a lot of long hours for little pay, going the extra mile, and finding ways to get your name out there so people with better gigs will give you a look. In between starting out and finding that "good job" is a whole lot of work. Time-consuming, all-encompassing and, if you're not careful, life-sucking work. To get it done, things got sacrificed.

For me, that meant any meaningful form of exercise, including all the wonderful free time I used to have to get outside. I found new thrills – beating deadlines, covering big stories, and getting some modest recognition – to keep my mind engaged, all while my body evolved in ways that weren't conducive to a long, healthy life. Oh, and I was still eating the same stuff, in the same quantities, as I did in college. The results were predictable. I was a 160-pound college kid. I turned into a 208-pound 28-year-old. There were times at night when I stressed out so much that I felt as if I were on the verge of a heart attack (yes, chest pains happened) and the clothes I was wearing had to be somewhat tent-like to fit.

You'd think that would be enough to bring me back around, but it would take another teacher to educate me on just how far I'd fallen.

****

The plan sounded fun. I've got a friend named Trent who used to be a youth minister at a church we attended in a small community east of Oklahoma City, and being a guy who is oriented toward the outdoors, Trent wanted to take his little band of teens on a hike in the Wichita Mountains of southwest Oklahoma. Then he asked me if I wanted to come.

Sure, I told him.

A little over a dozen of us piled into a fifteen-passenger van and motored southwest. We took off early as to avoid the brunt of the midday summer sun. A pit stop on the way there inspired me do an inventory of supplies, and I noticed a distinct lack of anything brought by the youth. So I bought a bunch of bottled waters and sports drinks and stuffed them into my backpack, knowing that somewhere on the trail, these kids were going to be thankful I was there, drink in hand, to save them from their ill preparedness. I was the "young man" of the group, younger than Trent, but older than the kids. I was not the leader, but in my mind, I saw myself being some sort of role model they could look up to. I'd be the epitome of strength and manhood and all that other crap. Why else would I be carrying this pack full of bottles, with the shoulder straps already digging into my skin?

I didn't know exactly where we were going that day, or how far, but it didn't matter. I'd handle whatever was thrown my way. As we pulled into the trailhead parking lot and piled out of the van, we started hiking up a solid trail toward the top of Elk Mountain, a huge mesa-like formation of granite that slopes gently uphill from the north, then heads back downhill on a rugged, steeper southern face. Just another walk in the park.

The hike up went pretty well. The walk isn't particularly steep or long – a gentle grade that goes on for about a mile until you top out on Elk Mountain's sizable summit, overlooking the wide valleys and pastures below to the north and the bouldery, jumbled and rugged canyon to the south. Tree cover is scarce, so as the sun rose, we absorbed its full force. It wasn't too bad, at least not yet, but with each hour the mercury rose.

Trent thought it would be fun to forgo the trail we ascended and instead do some boulder-hopping into the canyon below. From there, we'd explore some of the trails in the Charon's Garden Wilderness Area before heading back to the van.

The wilderness area's name has curious origins. Charon is a figure from Greek mythology. He's the boatman who ferries the dead across the River Styx and into Hades. Tradition had mourners put coins in the mouths of their dead to pay Charon's fare for the ride into the Underworld. There is no River Styx in Charon's Garden, but there is a Styx Canyon. And while going into Charon's Garden won't cost you any money, you might pay for it in other ways, particularly in the heat of summer. On that day, the sun continued to rise, unobstructed by clouds or trees, right on top of us. In Charon's Garden, there is more than one way to exact a toll.

So let's tally a few things up: It's now 100 degrees, we've got a mile of hiking to the top of Elk Mountain behind of us, and another few miles of hiking ahead. I'm about thirty pounds overweight. And on my back is a pack stuffed with bottled drinks, weighing God-knows-what.

Ring the bell, son. School's in.

Like I said, the ascent went fine. But as our group started down the other side of the mountain, hopping over boulders and absorbing more and more of the Oklahoma summer sun, bad things started to happen. Slowly – and inevitably – I started falling toward the back of the group. Then I was stopping every fifty feet just to catch my breath. Even the fat kid was leaving me in the dust.

Had this been a solo hike, I would have been in big trouble, especially since this was before the time when cellphones were ubiquitous. People have been evacuated from the Wichitas because they got lost, or cliffed out, or fell, or became so weak from heat exhaustion or dehydration that they couldn't continue.

Fortunately, I was not alone, and Trent could see what was up. He showed the patience necessary to give the kids the adventure he planned, while coaxing me forward to where I could finally collapse into the van and aim my face at the nearest air-conditioning vent.

Lesson complete.

The Wichita Mountains tested me and found me wanting. It was a humbling experience to be the weakest link in a group of people primarily composed of junior high kids with little to no experience in the outdoors. Six years removed from college and crashing through the brush and waist-high snow in Montana's Gallatin Range, I'd turned into a mushball barely capable of stumbling a few miles back to a trailhead parking lot, into a van, and ultimately, salvation from myself.

I had plenty of time to reflect on the day's events during the ride back home. Part of my problem, of course, was the heat. I was so concerned about making sure everyone had something to drink that I didn't bother to keep myself properly hydrated. But underlying that was the fact that I had neglected my own body for too long, too busy chasing the next good job and the next big story to understand that I was speeding toward obesity.

More importantly, I did so by shunning my outdoors self.

Things changed after that.

In the coming weeks and months, I rethought how I ate, how I exercised and where I was headed. I dropped the weight and wrestled my career ambitions into something less consuming and more sustainable. Over time, I discovered that a fitter me made for a guy who could do more and see more. The decade that followed may have been my best. All because of a hot summer day when I couldn't keep up with the fat kid.

But something more important occurred. It had been many years since I'd made any sort of habit of getting outside. Being out there again in a corpulent state was humbling, but also a homecoming. I felt that fitness as its own end was fine, but really, if you were going to whip yourself into shape, shouldn't there be some purpose to it? Otherwise wouldn't it just be another thing to do?

What if that newfound strength could haul you up a rock wall? If your heart, lungs and legs could propel you to the top of a mountain few others could reach? What if being as able-bodied as possible made it to where you could pick up and go anywhere in the world, load a big pack on your back, disappear for a week, and be just fine?

These thoughts set my wanderlust afire. The destinations I had in mind were the high places, the wild areas that were hard to get to, not always comfortable to be in, but beautiful and pure. These were the places you had to earn, but once you did, you'd feel compelled to return.

It would be a few years before I snagged my first high summit, a long hike through the alpine wilderness of the Sangre de Cristo Range that took me to a wide-open vista extending across northern New Mexico and into southern Colorado. It would be the first of many such trips, each one unique, times spent with good friends, beloved family members and folks who started out as complete strangers but became some of my favorite people on Earth. I'd learn a lot while exploring the wilderness in the Rockies and other places closer to home. The epiphanies gained through days of toil on the trail would be there for me in darker days marked by crises, tragedies and failures. Nature became my refuge, one that I'd need more and more as the years flew by.

The truth is, it had been there for me all along, all the way back to when I was a kid tromping through the woods or testing the waters in some remote mountain stream. I'd just forgotten. All I needed was a reminder, even if it was a harsh one. It's one that sticks with me on every run, hike or climb.

The outdoors will always be there for me. It might be harsh, indifferent, uncomfortable or dangerous. But in terms of its presence and availability, it is ever faithful.

TWO: ON THE RUN

"I always loved running...it was something you could do by yourself, and under your own power. You could go in any direction, fast or slow as you wanted, fighting the wind if you felt like it, seeking out new sights just on the strength of your feet and the courage of your lungs."

– Jesse Owens

Pulling into the trailhead parking lot, I realized the nice, easygoing run I planned was not going to happen. Something was charging through me, some weird energy. It wasn't anger, fear, frustration or anything like that. It was desire, a compulsion to leave it all out there, to test myself.

There is a park in Tulsa, a preserved wild space that is well known in the area for its mountain biking, hiking and running trails. It's hilly, rugged, wooded and quite frankly, one of the best natural resources the city has. It offers an escape for people who want an hour or five away from the worries of normal life.

When I moved here and started exploring this place, it was love at first sight. It's overrun with blackjack oak, carpeted with briars and grasses and inhabited by deer, rabbits, squirrels and snakes. Stony outcrops give you bird's-eye views of the Arkansas River to the east or nearby wooded ridges everywhere else. One perch even gives you a nice panorama of downtown Tulsa's skyscrapers six miles to the north. In the years since I first stepped foot here, I've trod almost every trail, either by hiking or running. Mostly running.

I usually take it easy during the early parts of my trail runs, mostly because I know a run of any length out here is going to include some big hills and rugged terrain that will wear me slick. But for whatever reason, on this day, I wanted hills. I wanted *all* the hills, starting with the first one, a steep, rocky pitch dubbed "Lipbuster" by the local mountain biking crowd (as in, going downhill on that stretch could send you over your handlebars and break your face wide open). It's a quarter-mile stretch that starts flat, then goes up just shy of one-hundred and forty feet. That's not a huge hill by trail running standards, but running it at the beginning is a little like starting your long run with a pace akin to a sprint.

I jogged along the flat stretch, then began the climb. My breathing became labored. My thighs began to burn. My body strained at the effort to scale that hill, being shocked into going from idle to maximum effort in a matter of seconds. It wasn't long before I topped out, turned left, and ducked into the trees on a gradual downhill that ended the first of many hill climbs to come. I was already breathing hard and feeling every step of Lipbuster's loose, rocky and steep path.

One might think that I'd regret the forthcoming sufferfest, especially with the knowledge of what lay ahead. But with the sounds of the breeze in the trees and the smells of honeysuckle filling my nose, it was anything but that.

I was having a ball.

****

I used to hate running. Every kid likes to run around all day, or ride their bikes or whatnot, but there came a point when I attained my adultish size that those pesky indoor habits took control. That's when running, whether for sports conditioning or just general exercise, got hard.

I ran for awhile with my dad in high school, mostly as a means to get in shape. I was a skinny little whip, and a few years of sitting on my butt playing video games had done nothing to make a man out of me. Some mileage at the local park seemed like a step in the right direction.

But after a time, those daily trips to the park wore on me. I didn't find the love for it a lot of people did, nor did I find a use for it in terms of helping other areas of my life. Instead, as a junior in high school, I discovered the weight room, and after a few weeks of pumping iron, I discovered my pecs.

When it comes to instant gratification, or something close to it, it's hard to beat that "pump" after a good lift. As the days turned into weeks, the stick-like frame of adolescence started packing on some bulk and an addiction was born.

Needless to say, I've been a gym rat ever since.

But weights as a cure-all for fitness are one-dimensional. Lifting is great and all, but there are some things that won't happen if all you do is lift.

What will happen, aside from bulking up, is you won't be able to last long on the basketball courts. You won't be able to run very far. Cycling becomes a chore. And unless your diet is dialed in, you're likely going to get fat. Gyms are filled with a lot of characters, and among them are really strong guys who are also a bit fluffy and are well on their way to dying young because they sport huge frames with sub-par cardiovascular systems. The idea of having a heart attack or stroking out is unnerving to me.

So I did what a lot of non-runners do. I cross-trained. Sort of.

There were cardio machines, but they were a last resort. I played basketball with co-workers and friends for years, and got a lot of benefits from that – great workouts, feeding my competitive urges, and gaining camaraderie with the dudes on the court. They didn't seem to mind that I wasn't very good. I was what you might call an "effort" guy.

In the midst of all that, I got into a job that gave me a once-a-week night shift that left me with some free time during the day. I saw this martial arts studio advertising jujitsu, and thinking that sounded pretty cool, I signed up without even knowing what it was. Seriously, the first time I heard the word was in *The Matrix* when Keanu Reaves' character, Neo, incredulously asked Tank if he was really going to learn jujitsu.

I wasn't so fortunate to have a computer download Royce Gracie's greatness into my brain. It took a while for it to stick, but stick it did. I did that for about seven years, and eventually became an assistant instructor. I met a ton of great people, learned about combat sports and found another way to stay in shape that did not involve running.

That's not to say I didn't dabble in running from time to time. Not long after my Elk Mountain debacle, I hit a stretch where I started running again, and I think that lasted a couple of months. Occasionally (maybe once every six months) I'd head out the door and lumber around the neighborhood. There were also times when basketball or jujitsu were on hiatus, so I'd force myself to do something, usually a mile or so of running at the park or at the track. It would feel good afterward, but not good enough to make me a runner.

Then life began to change. My job schedule altered radically, blowing up those lunchtime basketball games with my coworkers. The thought of jumping on an elliptical or a treadmill just crushed my spirit. One day after work I headed down to the gym, lifted weights for about an hour, and then peeked out the window. Within sight was a running path, not even a mile and quarter long, that wound its way around some small ponds and through a couple groves of oak and cedar. It was approaching dusk and the temps outside where somewhere in the sixties.

I looked at my options. The treadmill. The elliptical. The stairmaster. Then I looked outside again.

What the hell, I thought. I needed to be something, anything, other than a machine-bound cardio drone. So out I went.

And that, my friends, is when the magic happened.

The "trail" – really a concrete path with short and long loops – was deserted. As I started, little things popped out as I chugged along.

Turtles on the shoreline jumped into the ponds at my approach, then poked their tiny heads out of the water to see what I was doing. Ducks muttered muted quacks of protest as they paddled away on the water's surface. Sometimes I'd see some geese fly in on approach, their great wings spanning wide, then flapping hard for a gentle splashdown. All sorts of furry little friends were out rooting around in tall prairie grasses, and smaller birds darted through the skies feasting on an airborne buffet of bugs.

I made a turn back toward the trailhead, and from behind a small stand of cedars, there they were: four white-tailed deer, munching on grass and keeping a wary eye out for coyotes and people. They froze as I rounded the bend, then gracefully – and quickly – bounded away. The beauty of their athleticism stuck with me, burned into my memory in a way I can't explain, other than the fact that I know for certain I would not have enjoyed that moment had I stayed inside and succumbed to the contraptions designed to raise my heart rate while taking me nowhere.

I'd covered a little ground, man. I'd seen some things no one else got to see, at least not right then. I breathed clean air that didn't come from a vent. Aside from my own labored breathing and heavy footfalls, I heard absolutely nothing but birdsongs, duck calls and the persistent prairie winds blowing through the trees.

It was on that jogging path I found a small slice of peace. The solitude of the mountains I treasured so much, and yearned for so badly when I wasn't there, was right here all along. I didn't have to drive halfway across the country to find it. In a small way, that evening provided me an escape akin to a lifeline to a drowning man, but it was always present, ready to pull me out of the chaos every time I laced up my shoes and headed out the door.

That was the day I became a runner.

****

Trail running is a relatively new thing to me. When I moved to Tulsa, I used running as a way to explore the community. I heard about a place called Turkey Mountain and decided to give it a look.

First off, Turkey Mountain isn't really a mountain. It's more of a long, wooded ridge on the west bank of the Arkansas River. As a place, it's also not just one ridge, but several in what is properly known as the Turkey Mountain Urban Wilderness Area. The concept of an "urban wilderness" is not new; a scattering of cities have set aside green spaces that are left as close as possible to their natural state, with only some trails and a few signs giving folks directions. But it is rare in Midwestern and Southern Plains cities like Tulsa. Fortunately, city leaders and a few very wealthy benefactors set aside this slice of forested acreage to be kept wild. As such, it's an oasis for hikers, cyclists and trail runners seeking to flee the sameness of Tulsa's southern suburbs.

There is a lot of philosophical theory behind establishing wild places in the middle of cities, but on a practical side, Turkey Mountain offers a wide variety of terrain, dirt trails, nice hills and plenty of opportunity to challenge yourself in ways that pavement running cannot do. For nature freaks like me, it adds aesthetic qualities such as viewing wildlife, smelling wildflowers, and hearing the wind in the trees. The Rocky Mountains, the Appalachians, the Sierras, the Cascades – none of these great mountain ranges are outside my door. Yellowstone and Yosemite are several states away. In a state where there are almost no public lands and a whole lot of farms and ranches, a small patch of wild land like Turkey Mountain will have to do. But it's more than just a place I settle for. It's a rare gem, a nature escapist's urban dream, a small patch of earth that I've come to love.

Trail running is where I find everyday adventure, and in my city, those adventures happen at Turkey Mountain during a lengthy run over the park's rocky, rooty and hilly trails. Every city should have a place like this, somewhere with no paved paths, where you can lose yourself in the silence of the forest, see creatures on their terms, and earn every mile you traverse. In many communities, this is all the nature most people will ever see outside of a planned vacation or a PBS documentary. Places like Turkey Mountain can change lives. That might sound like hyperbole, but not when you hear stories like that of my friend Ken.

"The trails seem to give back," Ken told me when I asked about how he became a trail runner. Ken is a fixture in the local trail running scene, and knows Turkey Mountain better than anyone. I've learned a lot about the place running with him, and I've dubbed him the Dean of Turkey Mountain. He started out a bit like me, not liking the way he looked or felt, and he gave running a shot. After he ran his first 5K, he said, "I was hooked."

Ken plunged into all things running, then saw articles in magazines about trail running. He learned about Turkey Mountain through friends at a local sporting goods store and decided to check it out.

"I ran there once, got horribly lost, ran six miles – two more than I had ever run – and decided trails were my home." He and his wife liked it so much, they moved as close as they could to Turkey Mountain. Today, he's the owner of a few hundred-mile buckles from ultramarathons he's done, and he's the race director for six trail races in northeastern Oklahoma. And every Tuesday night and Sunday morning, he leads group trail runs on Turkey Mountain's earthen paths.

Years later, Ken hasn't lost that love and wonder of the woods.

"The exhilaration of flying through the woods with reckless abandon is magical. And the peaceful charm of going slow and drinking in each bend of the route, being greeted by twisted trees, touching wild flowers as you pass – it's so therapeutic. Every time out is different. I'm sort of a trail hound – always looking for new places to run.

"I really don't run much on roads. It kind of makes me happy to hear someone say they don't really like running on roads."

Upon topping out on Lipbuster, the route I chose graciously leveled off and headed down the ridge's west slope. The further down I went, the thicker the greenery, the more twisted the paths, the more technical the trails. Trees hugged the side of the trail, and given the ever-snakier nature of the route, my running started to resemble a downhill slalom, with blackjack oaks serving as gates as I sped down. The advancing spring made everything much more lush, meaning the trails looked almost new from week to week since the end of winter.

Somewhere along the way, I took a different turn. I broke through the trees into a small meadow. *"This looks new,"* I thought. But I was pretty sure something familiar would pop up soon. Back into the woods I ran, and then emerged to see something unexpected: a highway.

Somehow, after three years of running and exploring Turkey Mountain, I found a trail I'd never run before. The stretch was on the crest of an embankment about thirty feet above U.S. Highway 75, a busy thoroughfare running north-to-south through the city. Gone was the silence, overtaken instead by the steady drone of tires on pavement at sixty-five miles per hour. I figured I'd be turned off by this, but it was surprisingly cool: As people hurried along in their cars, I ran above them. It was a flat and pleasant stretch of singletrack far enough away from the road where I wasn't breathing in the fumes of traffic. I ran this for about a quarter-mile before the path ducked back into the woods and away from the highway.

Seeing something new is one of the greatest appeals of trail running. Each season, each day, each run brings something different. It's almost impossible to re-create that in a neighborhood. But on the trails, even on a day when you're not your best, something memorable is likely to happen.

This is what Ken meant when he described himself as a trail hound. Sniff around enough, you'll discover something that intrigues you and takes you on a new path to a pleasant unknown.

****

Something that struck me about running is how much you can learn about a town by exploring it on foot. Think about all the places you pass through in your car every day, and how little you really know about them. Glances as you pass by might give you snapshots of a neighborhood or its people, but it's doubtful you'd know much more about it than you would if you'd seen a thirty-second television report or a four-paragraph snippet in the news detailing something that happened there. You might get an impression, but not much more.

I tend to steer clear of designated running areas. Not that there's anything wrong with them, but going out my front door or outside my gym is a little more freeing. And more engaging.

I live and work in an urban area. So instead of being surrounded by row after row of rooftops, I find a sky broken up by early 20th century brick buildings and modern high rises that soar hundreds of feet into the air. I've long been a big fan of cityscapes, so my surroundings are eye candy to me – filled with landmarks, with new facets to be viewed on any given day.

A tour of my compact downtown brings with it an array of sights, sounds and smells. Not all of them are pretty, but most of them are interesting. I generally run without headphones, mostly because I like to take in every sensory detail that I can. Part of this is aesthetic, to be sure, but it's also a convenient distraction when fatigue and soreness begin to set in.

Running in the shadows of skyscrapers, old contrasts with new. Art-Deco architecture from Tulsa's first big oil boom adorn the streets like ornaments when sitting next to the looming office towers of more recent times. Cafes and restaurants cooking up barbecue, burgers, tacos or Asian foods lend a swirl of aromas that mix with the less pleasant stench of car exhaust. This miasma of scents is something you don't find in your typical neighborhood, and most people are OK with that. For me, however, it's just one ingredient in a fascinating sensory stew.

But what makes an urban place interesting are its people, and I get a kick out of people-watching, even when I'm plodding away at my nine-minute pace.

Starting out, I see a mix of professionals – lawyers, engineers, computer programmers and middle managers, dressed in sharp business attire and usually walking at a pretty good clip. Sitting quite still, usually on a park bench or on the ground, homeless folks in tattered clothes pass time asking for change, talking with each other, or sometimes talking to themselves. Many times, absent of anything to do or a place to go, they simply stare into space. If you're lucky, one of them might be strumming a guitar and singing a song, hoping their tune earns them a buck or two from passersby. Other times, they might be passed out, leaning against a building, wallowing in their own puke.

My path usually heads out from there and into a couple of entertainment districts, and the change of scenery brings with it a fresh set of people. Rehabbed old buildings have shucked their warehouse pasts and now don a new purpose, maybe that of a pub or a restaurant. Or perhaps an art gallery. Young people flock here, hipster guys sporting bushy beards, man buns and flannels – odd to most of us but cool in the eyes of this particular brand of fashion. Hipster gals in vintage clothing, colorful tats and smart-looking glasses are usually close by.

They're joined by a sizable crowd of people who are not "from here," visitors from the outskirts of town looking to catch a game at the downtown baseball stadium, cut a rug at a smoky dance club or catch some local bands jamming at any number of music venues. Depending on the day and time I go, I might run through quiet streets or thread my way through throngs of people.

Either way, it's going to be something new, and often, something intriguing.

On a few occasions, I even see other runners.

Most people don't say anything as I pass by, but a few do. I might get a "hey" when I make eye contact. On cold days some folks might comment how crazy I am for going out in shorts. But the best comments come from those homeless folks.

I had one guy ask me if I needed some change. Had to grin at that one. From another: "All that running, you need to run to Jesus!"

Amen, brother.

There are other things I've learned while on the run. Sometimes I'll take a route by the baseball stadium. It's a fairly new ballpark for Tulsa's Double-A baseball team, and it's a nice one at that. You can actually get good beer there (not just the swill most ballparks serve), and they shoot off fireworks at the end of Friday and Saturday night home games. Any seat in the house is good, with picturesque views of the downtown skyline clearly visible over the outfield wall.

The ballpark sits at the corner of Greenwood Street and Archer Avenue, once the nexus of what used to be called America's "Black Wall Street." Back before 1921, Tulsa's black community had built up some thriving enterprises just north of downtown. But an accusation was made – a black man assaulting a white woman, something that was never proven – and that set off an armed confrontation between white residents of the city and folks who lived in Tulsa's primarily black north side.

It was a bloodbath. The Tulsa Race Riot of 1921 left Black Wall Street a charred, broken ruin. An untold number of black-owned business and homes were burned, and while official figures on the number of dead are elusive, most historians put the body count in the hundreds. Black Wall Street was dead, and it died violently.

Northside residents rebuilt after the riots, trying to recapture the glory that the neighborhood once held. To an extent, they succeeded, but urban renewal projects, including a highway loop around downtown, razed many buildings and cut through the heart of the area. As the years passed by it degraded into a warehouse district with few tenants and high crime. In recent years it's been revived as an arts district, with lots of cool galleries, music venues, clubs, restaurants and bars. There's a hotel in there, too, and a great little park that's home to concerts, a farmer's market and people just hanging out or grabbing some grub from food trucks.

There's also that baseball stadium, and across the street from it, a smaller, less conspicuous park that was built to commemorate the losses of the Race Riot. It's called Reconciliation Park, and it's an incredible little green space. People who visit and take time to read the placards installed at various stations will get a chance to learn a few things about what were undoubtedly Tulsa's darkest days. It's great that we have this park; I wish it was bigger, maybe more dramatic, something befitting of all that was lost in 1921. I realize that doing so might have inconvenienced those who built the ballpark, the television station not far away, and all the trendy businesses nearby. I just hope everyone involved in the establishment of these places understands their prosperity is built on the ashes of someone else's long-ago broken dreams. The Tulsa Arts District is a jewel for my city, alive with people and commerce. But that was also true of Black Wall Street in 1921. It just so happened that back then the people who flocked here were of a different hue than the rest of the city, a fact leaving them relatively powerless to stop the nightmare that burned the heart of their community to the ground.

I usually run through that park at least a few times a week. I make a point of it.

Not everything I've seen or learned during these jaunts has been so somber. Mostly, it's allowed me to become more intimately familiar with the community where I live. People living in more walkable cities like New York already know this to be true. The rest of us living in communities beset by urban sprawl are left to learn about our hometowns through those quick glances out a car window or blips on the news, our cities and even our neighborhoods neatly and efficiently compartmentalized, isolated from places as close as a half-mile away. No wonder we don't often know our own neighbors.

I've mentioned that the best moments of running for me come on the trails, and that's definitely true. But there are ways all those runs on the streets and on dirt intersect. Trail running is all about engaging your senses, taking part in an exercise of exploration. The same is true of my "urban trails." I lived in a small town for more than twenty years at one point. When I moved, I learned more about my new city in a fraction of that time solely based on the fact that I took the time to explore it on foot.

Where those urban and dirt trails diverge (aside from the obvious setting, of course) is in mood. The city is often information overload. Dirt trails are simplicity. The city moves fast. The woods are mostly still. Shiny objects, passing vehicles, glowing signs and other distractions vie for your attention in a city. On the dirt, the pull is much more subtle and kind. Cities invite you to engage. The trails invite you to just be. When you're out running those grassy hills or wooded single tracks, you don't have to shut out the surroundings. You can actually take time to absorb the aroma of the forest, the contours of the trees, the colors of the rocks. When you explore a city, you take quick mental notes. When you explore trails you let the mind out of its cage. So as much as I love and need my urban trails, they'll always take a back seat to running in a hilly forest, dirt underfoot, jumping over rocks and roots and bounding down a slender, snaking path of earth that leaves me wondering what's around the bend.

The likes of Walt Whitman, Henry David Thoreau, John Muir and Ansel Adams knew this well. We can live and prosper within the constructs of men. But we thrive in the environs of God.

****

By now, I'd spent the last couple of miles weaving through tree-lined paths, over rocks, under tree limbs, into ravines and up hillsides. The weather was still fine, the temperature perfect. I was getting a good sweat as I finished off a steep climb and broke through the trees. When I emerged, I looked at what lay before me: a mile-long straight shot south through a clear-cut strip that makes room for a long row of power lines. Under those electrified steel towers is what amounts to an old jeep road.

There's no shade here, and if you choose to run, hike or bike this stretch, there's no break either. The Powerline Trail does you no favors by its direct route south, mostly because it goes straight down one hill, then straight up another.

I've run this piece many times. It's much easier going north than it is south. But today, I've got to go south to finish my loop.

It wasn't hard at first, a moderate downhill that lasts about a quarter mile before bottoming out near a couple of ponds. At the base of the next hill is the wreckage of an old white pickup. I don't know the story of how it got there, but whatever happened, it left that pickup a crumpled, battered mess. The thinning paint and growing rust tell me it's been there awhile, and judging the terrain down there, it's not going anywhere anytime soon.

It's also a bit foretelling. I knew when I got through running the next mile or so, I might feel a bit like that truck. Three steep uphill pitches awaited. Running up hills like this isn't everyone's thing, that's for sure. It would be hard. I'd end up winded. I'd want to quit.

But up I went.

The sun beat down on me as I tackled that first pitch. It wasn't bad, but I was feeling it. The path leveled out for about a hundred yards, and then came the steepest, longest and toughest part of the climb. I dove in.

The steps became shorter, choppier. Try as I might to regulate my breathing, it was no use. I huffed and puffed like no one's business. With several miles already under my belt, my legs started burning, especially my thighs. When the trail finally relented, it felt like my heart might burst from my chest at any moment. I couldn't breathe deep enough or fast enough to recoup. The trail dipped down slightly for another hundred yards or so, but the third and final pitch loomed. It's steep, sandy, rocky and downright ugly. And there's no way through it but up.

It's here where it's easy to stop, put your hands on your knees and give in to the suffering. Maybe take five, then hike the rest before solemnly heading back down again. It's understandable. There's nothing comfortable or particularly fun about what I was doing right then. But in a weird way, there was something important going on.

I had to make a choice. Would it be hands-on-knees? Or would I embrace the discomfort? Would I look up at the sun, duck into the trees and choose an easier way out? Or would I push through, regardless of how it made me feel, and see where the pain train took me? What would I gain if I did? What would I lose if I didn't?

I pressed on. I embraced the suffering, the elements, chugging slowly, ungracefully up that hill. Gravel spat out from under my feet. Rocks rolled to the right and left. I pumped my arms to get a little momentum going, but the ascent was still slow. In time, that last steep slope gave way to a gentler incline. The top was near, and my body was grateful. I was totally gassed. This hill wouldn't be a big deal to most ultramarathoners, but to everyday schmoes like me, it's really damn hard. I topped out, turned left and darted into the trees. The run was almost over, and it was quite literally all downhill from here. I let gravity do the work, basically moving my legs as I headed down.

On this day, I passed the test. I took on a challenge, minor as it might be, pushed through the pain and came out on top. I wasn't smiling on the outside, but I was grinning like a Cheshire cat from within. In a weird way, I was having fun.

****

"Pain is weakness leaving the body."

"Embrace the elements."

"Enjoy the sufferfest."

I'm sure most runners of any distance longer than a couple of miles have had similar thoughts or quotes roll through their minds as the miles pile up and fatigue sets in. A lot of us chase after the elusive "runner's high" that people talk about, but really, it only hits me when it's over and the endorphins kick in. In between those first few steps and finishing up lies varying stages of discomfort caused by respiratory stress, muscle fatigue, joint soreness and whatever the weather is offering that day.

One thing I've found to be true is you can't run faster or longer until you learn the concept of accepting discomfort. I'm not talking about injuries or illness. This is referring to the times when your breathing is labored, your muscles are done, and you have a ways to go to reach your goal. Pain becomes a constant companion. If it's going to be with you the entire way, you may as well make peace with it.

An analogy I like to make is with boxing. You can learn a lot of cool moves, you can hit a bag or target mitts for days and weeks and months on end. But at some point, you have to step into the ring against another person, knowing full well you're going to get punched in the face. And then you have to take that hit. Some people find out quickly that boxing ain't for them. But for those who can shrug it off, stay in the ring and keep punching, that threshold opens the door to becoming a fighter.

Though not exactly the same, running is similar.

Most people can "run" a mile. They may have to run/walk it, and it may be really slow, but getting a mile under your belt is very doable for average, able-bodied people.

But the number drops off quite a bit when the distance hits three miles. Even more at 10. Half marathon? Now we're talking a fraction of a fraction. And those numbers get smaller as the mileage ramps up.

There are a lot of reasons for this, but the biggest is that it's hard. If you're in shape, a solid five-miler can be taxing but fun. But I don't know many people who finish a full marathon and say, "Boy, let's do that again next week!" A few crazies, sure. But we mere mortals finish that 26.2 tired, hurting and glad it's done.

There is an allure to doing it, however. The idea of taking on a challenge and then accomplishing it has a strong pull. Once you cross the finish line after 26.2 miles you enter a club that is reserved for a few tough-minded people that is, statistically, very rare among the general population. It's a bucket list thing for a lot of people, running's version of a black belt, I suppose. I remember the thought rolling around in my head after my first marathon, echoing for days, *I can't believe I just did that.*

But more important than the finish line is the process of getting there.

Doing pilgrimages used to be a thing for people ages ago, back when a journey of hundreds or even thousands of miles was something to be done on foot over the course of many months. The destination was usually a place with some sort of religious significance, and it took great perseverance and resourcefulness just to get there. But the tales of those pilgrimages often carried similar themes of how a person was changed not by the place where they were going, but by the experiences collected along the way.

It's the same way with running.

I've got a lot of marathon memories, but they aren't as vivid as all those speed drills, the runs through pouring rain, the long training sessions of fifteen, eighteen, or twenty miles. The cumulative experience, pain and growth that occurred over a twenty-one-week period before race day is what made that finish happen, while also teaching me what was possible, and what is still out there to achieve. I'd like to say that all those weeks of training were filled with joy and strength, and positive, affirming, rainbow-farting-unicorns-in-green-pastures good vibes. But the truth is I spent that time in a constant state of fatigue. My feet, knees, hips and back hurt. I'd lose sleep thinking about the weekly long run, particularly as the day drew closer. There were bad runs where I constantly doubted myself, wondering how in the world I'd polish off a marathon when sixteen miles seemed so impossibly hard.

But in the midst of that, something builds. Maybe not confidence, but determination. One more mile. Keep moving forward. It doesn't have to be pretty or fast, just forward. Don't quit. Finish the job. Rest. And then meet the new challenge of the week. In a way, this is how toughness is made. And part of being tough is the ability to embrace discomfort, and do so for as long as it takes to complete the task at hand. You learn a lot about yourself in times like these, but you also change a lot about yourself.

Some folks would call the marathon a metaphor on life, and that's true. But for me, there is more to it than that. This is going to sound strange, but there is something to be enjoyed in the midst of suffering, or at least in the kind of suffering endurance sports impart.

I see this not just from the length of a run, but in the conditions you run in.

This is a big deal to me. My aversion to the treadmill or the indoor track puts me outside in all seasons and conditions. This gets interesting in the summer.

Where I live, it gets hot. Not Arizona hot, but pretty hot. It can be muggy. There are times when I'm faced with a choice: Do I go outside and hit those trails when the temps are spiking over a hundred degrees, or do I just pop into a spin class instead? Both will be tough, but the indoor workout will be far less miserable than a jaunt into the Oklahoma summer blast furnace.

Almost without fail, however, I'm headed out the door.

A few summers ago, we were in the midst of a nasty heat wave and drought conditions that spawned record high temperatures. I drove to the trailhead, air conditioning in my little Honda going full blast, and then shut the car down. I checked the temperature. It was one-hundred and ten degrees.

I did all the things I needed to do to get ready for this workout, but the real game was in my head. I knew I would not go fast or far. I'd just go. I won't lie, a lot of things about that run sucked. But there were silver linings.

When the weather is nice, the trails are busy. But when it's a hundred-and-ten? The trails are empty.

I'm one of those guys who enjoys a little solitude, and nothing will make a place more lonely than an inhospitably hot day. I had a couple of hours when there was almost no one on the trails. No distractions. Just me and the overheated woods on a bright, broiling summer day.

I enjoy running with people, and I find it empowering to see others getting out there and getting it done. But it's also special to be out there in the woods and the only other human is miles away. The place looks and sounds different when the only footfalls you hear are your own. There are no voices. You stop, take a break and catch your breath, and the things you notice are the breezes in the trees, bird calls, cicadas and the occasional squirrel or lizard scurrying away through the leaves. This is an amazing way to clear your head.

The same can be said in the winter. I like running in the cold. I feel faster, and the cold doesn't zap me like the heat does. I'm not saying that going out when it's fifteen degrees is more fun than it is on a sunny, sixty-degree day, but it has an allure of its own.

Sometimes we get some decent snow, though not often. When it happens, I want to get out in it.

When you live in the flatlands, the cold has the same effect on people as the heat, as it drives people indoors. There aren't any ski slopes where I live.

Adverse weather conditions provide the same results when it comes to the trails in that a snowy, icy day empties them out just like a hundred-degree day.

On one memorable run, when a fresh coat of snow and ice hit the city, I bundled up, stepped out and found my way to the trailhead on a gray, overcast and still day.

I think I saw one other runner out there that day. A hiker or two. But mostly, the woods were devoid of people. It was eighteen degrees outside. Snow carpeted the forest floor and adorned the now-leafless branches of blackjack oak.

The quiet was what made an impression on me. Wildlife had hunkered down, conserving heat and energy. The only sound I heard was the crunching of snow and ice under my feet. I stopped every now and then just to soak it all in.

Those dark, twisted tree limbs contrasted starkly with the snow on the ground and the deepening gray of late afternoon cloud cover. All was still.

The bracing cold, the crunchy snow, and the peace of a woodland cloaked in white is, as one of my friends described it, "magical." It makes me a little jealous of the people who get snowy conditions more often than we do down south. I know there are downsides. But in that moment, when you're out there in the midst of a wintertime sensory feast, you don't think about the downsides. The chill doesn't bother you. Rather, the sights, the smells, and the silence feed your soul. God paints in many colors, and sometimes even the muted and stark shades of winter are stunning when laid out on the canvas just so.

These two very different scenes unfolded before me on days that were decidedly uncomfortable. And yet, what would I have missed had I not gone out? Not every run is going to happen on a mild, bluebird day. But each day offers opportunities to see and experience something new. The more you get out there, the better your chances of seeing it happen.

Over the past several years, I've seen a lot of interesting things that never would have happened on an elliptical, churning my legs on a spin bike, or clomping along on a treadmill. The price for admission: embracing some pain, enduring some cold, putting up with the heat. Suffering a little to gain a lot. Our days are numbered, you know, and nothing good is really free.

****

As the trail headed downhill, I slowly regained my breath. By now I was tired, but in a pleasant way. Sunlight washed over me in between the shadows of the trees. I was dodging rocks and jumping from spot to spot as the trail steepened. A few stretches like that, and I bottomed out. The path flattened and turned into a friendly surface of earth made kinder by recent rains. There was a sense of relief that the route was almost complete, that the work was nearly done. Just a quarter mile to go.

But part of me was sad to see it end. I had some juice left in the tank. I pondered this as I hit the last final stretch, passing by casual hikers with families, or folks walking their dogs. Finally I broke through the trees and reached the trailhead parking lot. I slowed to a walk, hands on my hips, and breathed deep.

One of the things that appeals to me about running – whether it's out here on the trails or in the middle of a busy cityscape – is each outing is like a little adventure, at least if you open your eyes and drink in the surroundings. Not everyone leads a life where they can step outside and boom – a new outdoorsy adventure awaits. Even to the people who dedicate their lives to living adventurously, those really incredible experiences in wild places, in new cultures, in faraway places, are often small bites of time in between working odd jobs, hours on the road or otherwise mundane stretches that are anything but exciting.

But the fact remains that even the most settled of us needs an escape. Some need it more than others, and I think I'm part of the group that needs it more. But what do you do if you live in a place outside those exotic tropical beaches, or far from soaring mountains? How do you cope?

Well, I run. As much as I benefit from it physically, running also engages my mind in a strikingly similar way that climbing a big mountain or hiking a scenic trail does. For a time – be it twenty minutes or several hours – I get a tiny escape from ordinary life to shut my mouth and listen to the world around me. I get to cover some ground and see things in an intimate way that you can't do online, on TV or inside a car. That sort of mental engagement, when mixed in with a few endorphins, is one tasty treat.

I found myself in that parking lot. It was a beautiful day. The sun was shining. I still had some energy in my legs, a little time on my hands, and at the other end of the lot is a trailhead for a short little loop through a different part of the woods. It was only another mile. So why not? The fun didn't have to end quite yet. So off I went. I've been given so many minutes and hours in this life. Might as well spend them well.

THREE: ROAD TRIPPIN'

"Nothing behind me, everything ahead of me, as is ever so on the road."

— *Jack Kerouac*

There are some who say true adventure is dead. There are not many peaks left unclimbed, forests unsurveyed and deserts untraversed. With satellite technology, we've pretty much quantified all the lands of the earth, leaving behind few hidden worlds to be discovered.

Worse still is that life in the modern, developed world actually shuns adventure. Our lives are routine, regimented and fenced-in. Show me someone whose life is mostly outside this realm and, most likely, you'll be looking at a homeless vagabond.

So let's face a few facts: We like predictability. Societally-induced quality control. We all color inside the lines, and whether we admit it or not, we gravitate toward sameness. Too much variation from our scheduled, hurried lives is unsettling, and yet life spent inside that manicured slice of stability can be stifling. Why has the film "Office Space" turned into an enduring classic comedy? Because it pokes fun at the lives most of us lead. Those soul-crushing, mind-numbing hours spent every day for five days a week in which we toil inside cube farms to enjoy the same two days off. During those days off, we do the same chores around the house, in the yard or, if we're feeling ambitious, gathering with friends at a club, movie theater or backyard grill. We could spend decades doing this and never lack for anything and yet still feel like we've accomplished nothing.

That's why middle-aged men buy $20,000 motorcycles and ride in groups to Sturgis, or why 40-something women join the teenage concert crowd with their gal pals and rock out like it was 1989. It's why we take up skydiving, scuba or ballroom dance. Or whatever it is that stands so far apart from what we do every day that people simultaneously gawk at and envy us for attempting something so beyond the norm. This is what we do when the need to break free becomes too pressing to ignore. In that way, it's the definition of "escape."

"Escape" can also be about leaving the place you're at, physically removing yourself from the fences that enclose your home, and going somewhere – anywhere – else. And that is why the road trip is so quintessentially and perfectly American: Pointing to a place on the map, gassing up the car and saying, "I'm going here. See you in a couple of weeks." Modern adventure, for most of us, is partly about escaping the world in which we're comfortable, or maybe getting away from a place we're no longer comfortable in at all.

We can thank several people for the concept of the American road trip. Henry Ford made cars affordable for working stiffs like you and me. A whole slew of entrepreneurial souls birthed the amalgam of attractions that gave life to the Mother Road, Route 66, the ribbon of pavement that fueled dreams of wanderlust. And of course, President Eisenhower later endowed the nation with the interstate highway system. Our country is huge, diverse and wide open. You can drive for days at highway speeds and not traverse its expanse. Within it are numerous mountain ranges, wide rivers, deep gorges and glimmering cities. Endless miles of open prairie are only outdone by even more endless miles of farmlands that feed the world. America is peopled with energetic go-getters, stodgy blue bloods, hopeless curmudgeons and weirdos. Every state has a bit of everything – hippies and rednecks are ubiquitous. Jump in your car or on your bike and if given the time, you can see it all, see *them* all.

When I think about road trips I recall the movie *Animal House*. One of the best parts was the Delta boys' roadie in which they landed in a club where they were clearly not welcome, then faced the prospect of a huge, angry man standing over them, menacingly asking, "May we dance with your dates?" They bolted from the joint in terror, laughing it up only as they sped safely away, tires squealing. Had that been you, would you not relive that moment every time you got together with your old college buddies? I know I would.

The reason is because that *Animal House* road trip is, in its own way, a tale of adventure. It's not hanging from a rock face 2,000 feet in the air with a swirling blizzard all around, but still out of the ordinary, foreign and risky, one might even say exhilarating. A tale retold amongst friends for as many years as you gather, still inducing the imagery, scents and emotions that first hit you when you were living it. We go on the road to find ourselves, or maybe lose ourselves, getting out there to build a new story that goes beyond the cubicles and seven-foot privacy fences.

****

Several years back I made it a point to make road trips a more regular part of my life. Taking to the road is one of the few outlets I have to really break free, and it sure beats the cost and hassle of flying. It helps that I'm within driving distance of some truly great places. Even better, I've even been able to convince a few friends to join the fun.

On one such venture, four of us gathered in a parking lot shortly after work, our cars stuffed with camping and fishing gear, ready to escape the mid-summer Oklahoma heat for a few days and trade it for cooler, crisper air deep in the Rockies. We'd arranged to borrow a church's fifteen-passenger van for the trip – overkill, considering there were only four of us. But it would be a nice luxury to haul ourselves and all our stuff and still have plenty of room to stretch out, spread out, sleep or whatever.

There are differing philosophies as to when to start a long road trip – first thing after work, and drive through the night, or first thing the next morning. A lot of the guys I've traveled with grew up heading west to ski, and in hoping to get as much time as possible on the slopes, they'd travel overnight before stumbling into the ski resort the next morning. This was that kind of crew.

All of the guys had gone with me and several other fellas on a backpacking trip into the mountains the year before. There were 10 people on that trip. My guess is that backpacking isn't for everyone, but it was all good with these hardy souls.

Rick had been with me on two of these trips. We met my brother Mike in New Mexico to go hike up that state's highest mountain, and then the next year, when our merry band of inexperienced but happy backpackers tried to tackle the steep challenges of the Collegiate Peaks of central Colorado.

Rick is one of those quietly intense people who is all smiles and mellow vibes when you meet him. But he's a deep thinker, very spiritual, and unafraid of diving "deep into the rabbit hole," as he likes to say. If you're going to get into a serious discussion about life or philosophy with Rick, hold on tight, brutha. Get ready for a lengthy tour of Wonderland.

He's also strong as a bull, and as he puts it, big enough of a boogerhead to gut his way through just about anything. That's the perfect type of person to take on an alpine backpacking trip.

Jeff is another longtime friend, a guy whose outdoor accomplishments were far greater than mine, and one of the more well-rounded people I've ever known. Jeff grew up in a small Oklahoma town called Seminole. He played football, worked tough jobs, met the lady of his dreams and settled into a life that took them to places like Crested Butte and Telluride before heading back to Oklahoma and raising their growing family.

Jeff skis better than me. Better than most people I know, actually. He's very much the aesthete, which explains why he prefers telemarking to downhill, and loves fly fishing even if nothing is biting. He hunts game birds in the fall, became an RN, and is as intelligent, spiritual, and sincere as anyone I know. He is just as comfortable in a deep conversation over coffee at a trendy café as he is on the back of a tractor. He's a pretty smart redneck.

Oh, and the dude can sing. He plays guitar and plinks around on a piano, too, but I've often said the stars of "The Voice" or "American Idol" couldn't hold a candle to the pipes he's packing. He earns his money in a hospital, but his life is expressed far more fully when he's leading worship at his church or sitting in a ring around a fire with friends belting out tunes for hours. I'm not kidding when I say he's the biggest undiscovered vocal talent in the country right now, and that's just the way he prefers it. I think he'd much rather be on that tractor or stuck behind a duck blind than living the life of a rock star, playing arenas and becoming the next big social media superstar. He'd rather be at home with a very select group of people, never does anything on Facebook and will half-jokingly tell you "Come back when you can't stay so long" when the hour gets late.

And then there's Trent. He's another one of those guys who is better at just about everything outdoorsy than me. I've learned a whole lot about backpacking and camping by watching him. He's a stout climber and ran a ropes course at a huge Baptist youth camp for several years. Back in the day, he was into competitive cycling and was quite good.

He's a teacher by trade. He's also been a youth minister, but backed away from that when he was criticized for reaching out too often to the down-and-out kids and not the team captains and cheerleaders of the world. Trent and his wife own some acreage in rural Oklahoma where they raise horses, ducks, goats and a whole slew of other animals, and I can attest from personal experience that he's a fine home brewer. He's well-read, good natured and deep. It makes sense that he likes "The Lord of the Rings," because he's a real-life mash-up of many of its characters. He's simultaneously Gandalf and Aragorn, moving effortlessly between Gimli and Frodo. If you're not nerdy enough to understand that then you might not get Trent, but he'd grow on you just the same. Trent is not the guy you'd expect to be a leader. But he ends up becoming one because people gravitate toward him when he reluctantly holds court.

All of these guys are a little older than me. In their presence, I feel the least capable, the shallowest, the weakest link, but that's just where I want to be when I'm hitting the road. This is the kind of crew I want to hang with during those long hours on the highway, those tough stretches on the peak, and in times of reflection.

Road trips can be transformative. If that's important to you, the company you keep is crucial.

So we hauled our stuff into the van and piled in. The setting sun baked the road and glared at us as we got on the highway, pointing our rig roughly in the direction of the Rockies, still a few hundred miles away. The mountains were on my mind, but as the next several days unfolded, the peaks were just a setting for something far better.

****

I have a personal philosophy when it comes to road trips: They should always begin by getting in your car/truck/rig, and pointing that sucker west. Let me explain...

Not long ago, I was sitting around with a bunch of co-workers as we wished a colleague well during his last days with us. He was leaving to take a job in Pittsburgh, which to me seems like a far-off place in a totally different world from my current home in Tulsa.

Someone asked him if he'd be driving straight through or stopping overnight. He chose the latter, but said the trip can be made in about fifteen or sixteen hours.

That shocked me. So many states away, and it's just sixteen hours from here?

That's only two hours longer than my last trip to western Colorado, that big rectangular mass that actually borders my home state.

It got me thinking about the vastness of the West, the wonderful, weird, wide open expanse of what I think is best in America.

A few hours earlier, I was home watching a re-run of Anthony Bourdain's *No Reservations* program. It was one of my favorite episodes, the one where he hangs out with Queens of the Stone Age's Josh Homme in the high desert of California. In addition to the coolest soundtrack of any show on TV, it showed more of what makes the West so alluring to me: Desperate scenes of civilization clinging to life on the shores of the Salton Sea, a dude who painted a mountain (literally painted on the whole mountain) and long stretches of open highway slicing through arid wastelands most people would assume avoid.

Vast, wonderful, weird and wide-open.

Where I live, in my opinion, is sort of the dividing line between east and west. Tulsa is right on the edge of the Ozarks, which I see as being Appalachia lite. Drive a few hours west and you're in the high plains. At the edge of that, you hit the Rockies.

That's where things get interesting.

I was born in Illinois and have lived most of my life in Oklahoma, but I grew up in Colorado. Despite this pesky accent I've picked up I consider myself a westerner. To this day, I still envision sunsets over the Rockies and associate pines with the high country.

This had an effect on me. I live here in T-town, but feel compelled to return to what in my mind is my homeland. It's sort of a salmon-spawning-grounds story, but without the whole breeding/dying/getting-eaten-by-bears thing. Money (or a lack thereof) keeps me from going more often. To be honest, I've got a serious road trip itch working right now.

My pilgrimages there have often been with friends and family. A couple of times, they've been blessedly solo. However it works, the one thing that is true is that I feel a little more free when I go. Sometimes dangerously so, or at least that's how it seems – on your own, the comforts of home farther and farther away, but the promise of seeing something new and possibly transformative pulling you down the road. Road-tripping is the best form of American escapism there is, and the West is a magnet for dreams of freedom.

And it always has been. Since the founding of the nation, people have looked west to find their destiny or otherwise flee the confines of the lives into which they were born.

That's one of the most interesting aspects of the West. Free spirits, non-conformists, weirdos and outlaws all looked to the wilderness beyond the Mississippi. The profound impact this has had on the American cultural landscape can't be understated.

I've often told people that the farther west in America you go, the weirder it gets. Boulder is pretty weird. All those little mountain towns from Montana to New Mexico are pretty weird (even the smallest Montana villages have at least one church and one bar). Roswell is weird. In Nevada, you get the weirdness of Las Vegas, Burning Man and Area 51 within its odd confines. Once you hit the coast, you reach the gleaming metropolises of Los Angeles, San Francisco, Portland and Seattle. The farther you make your way west and north, the stranger it gets.

And then there's Alaska. For those fleeing conformity, broken relationships, the law or any other demons, there is no farther place you can go, at least not in the U.S. You have to be committed to go that far, and even more so to stay. And that makes for a place with some truly colorful personalities – real frontiersmen and women who could actually live libertarian ideals of self-sufficiency, and ex-governors who say they can see Russia all the way from suburban Anchorage.

People go to these places, and invariably, those places change them. A person who has lived in the mountains or the desert for any length of time won't look, talk, think or act like those who have spent their existence in a suburb of Cincinnati or in a borough of New York. Harsher climes and sweeping landscapes alter people in that way, building up quiet strength and self-reliance while stripping away pretense. Scratching out a living out West will humble and toughen you in ways few other places can. Many folks envy that, which explains why people pay for the privilege of spending a week on dude ranches and will even shell out thousands to outfitters who give them "authentic" backpacking experiences. Guns are scary to many Americans; they're just tools to the people of the rural West.

And let's revisit that landscape. America is filled with gorgeous places. I've been out east quite a bit. Tennessee, Pennsylvania and West Virginia are knockout beautiful. Closer to home, northwest Arkansas has the same feel. All throughout the east you have these wonderful hills and mountains, thick woods and meandering rivers.

But it's also stable. It feels old. Established. And that makes sense, seeing that the communities in the east date back to the 1600s or even earlier, and the Appalachians are some of the most ancient mountains on Earth.

Not so much in the West. While some Spanish settlements there are quite old, most cities and towns out West are pretty new, historically speaking. The mountains themselves are younger. Their rise is more dramatic, and in the case of the Tetons, startlingly so. The West has volcanoes. One of them famously blew up back in 1980, and we know that some of its Cascadian neighbors could well do the same. The West has glaciers. In one section of Colorado, deep in the San Juans, you can see the confluence of geologic uplift, volcanism and ice-age glacial carving, sculpting a landscape so wild that it boggles the mind.

Wind gives us the carefully crafted arches and towers of Utah and Arizona. A tiny alpine trickle gathers itself and plummets downhill, gaining strength and size and speed until it slices a gash so long, wide and deep that it can be seen from space.

Towering heights.

Deep canyons.

Deserts and rain forests. Grizzly bears, wolves, eagles and whales.

Is there any wonder as to why I don't take off right now?

I envision a future trip unfolding like so many others have in the past: I'm in my car, cruising at seventy-five miles per hour on a two-lane highway with endless vistas of the Oklahoma Panhandle prairie all around. The stereo is up loud, cranking out tunes from U2's *The Joshua Tree*. In the back, with the seats down, my belongings – a pack, a tent, food, mountaineering gear and campsite tools – jostle with the contours of the road.

Then I spot it. Rabbit Ear Mountain, a small peak in the far northeastern corner of New Mexico, a marker of what I see as the easternmost outpost of the Rockies.

I grin a bit. Adventure is close. And I keep driving.

West.

****

Usually when we plan a road trip, the destination is the sales pitch. Back in college, it was skiing, or maybe hitting the highway to go to some far-off lake for some fishing or camping. For someone to go with you in a car for several days, there needs to be a draw that makes it worthwhile.

The pull for our trip was twofold. We'd had a pretty good time in Colorado camping in Missouri Gulch Basin and doing a summit hike of Mount Belford, so we figured, why not do something like that again? Our only disappointment from that trip was not finding any decent fishing. So Jeff got in touch with some buddies living in Gunnison and learned of a place on the Gunnison River, deep in the Black Canyon, where there were rumors of waters that actually held real live fish.

So goal No. 1: Hit the summit of Mount Elbert, Colorado's highest peak and the second-highest point in the lower forty-eight states at 14,433 feet. Goal No. 2: Go into the Black Canyon, scramble around the rocks for a bit and get a hook wet in the fast-flowing waters of the Gunnison.

If you're not familiar with it, Mount Elbert is not one of those mountains that conjures up epic feats of mountaineering. For all its lofty heights, it's strictly a hike, a walk-up peak that takes a strong heart, lungs and legs, but that's about it.

My memories of Mount Elbert are pretty simple. There are multiple false summits, which is annoying as hell when you're dead tired and ready to stop going up. The thought of bagging it and going down passed through my mind a couple of times. But then I would have missed out on Trent tossing a snowball at me from the summit, hearing the sounds of young ladies singing hymns at the top (beautiful, but really, I can't freaking breathe and you all are singing?), and looking down on Twin Lakes more than 4,000 feet below.

I also learned something. When using bug spray, resist the urge to rub it all over your face. When you sweat, the spray will run down your cheeks and nose and into your mouth. Bug spray tastes horrible and it will make your lips numb. Trust me on that one.

We got off the mountain, packed up camp and headed out to the town of Gunnison, where Jeff had arranged for us to meet up with a couple of his buddies who were familiar with the canyon and where the fish were. You can drive to the bottom, and there are decent campsites up and down the banks of the Gunnison River. But most of the easy places to fish are all fished out. You want to catch something in the Gunnison? You're going to have to earn it. That's where Jeff's friends came in handy.

The plan was to hike the shoreline for less than a mile, then cross the river to get to the other bank. From there, we hiked a little more until confronted by a large rock buttress that you cannot go around. You either climb up and over or stop dead in your tracks.

It's a loose dirt scramble (there was some rockfall, and we dodged one toaster-sized stone that got kicked loose) until you get to the top. Your crux move ends up being a blind bouldering move in which you secure some handholds and footholds and, with a more committing move, swing over to reach the next handhold. It's not too hard, but you don't want to miss. Otherwise, it's a 100-foot tumble to the river below. Having a pack on my back with my tackle, pole and a pair of waders made it a little more interesting, but the fishing that followed was worth the risk.

I like to fish, but angling for trout in streams goes way beyond that. Reading the river, ascertaining where the fish are going to be, and then casting in has all the same allure as looking at a previously never-seen crag, figuring out a line and then climbing it. Each crack is different, just like each bend in the river. It's a puzzle, both physical and mental, but one-hundred percent aesthetic. The satisfaction of topping out on a challenging pitch is not much different than feeling that sharp tug on your line when a trout hits your lure and fights to wriggle free. At least that's how it feels to me. Maybe I need to climb harder stuff, but there is something to be said about the excitement and gratification of reeling in a nice fish surrounded by the beauty of a river that flows through the dramatic and colorful cuts of an ancient Rocky Mountain canyon.

Most of us did pretty well that day. All of us had fun. I didn't haul in any trophies, but that was easily one of the most memorable fishing experiences I've ever had.

As vivid and pleasant as all these memories were, however, they took a back seat to the rest of the trip. And by "the rest of the trip," I mean the time we spent going from place to place in that sky-blue, fifteen-passenger van.

By then, my brother Mike, who had joined us on Mount Elbert, had taken off to get back to Denver, his family and his job. Unlike the rest of us, he hadn't been able to push off the real world for a week. So that left the four of us, our gear rustling around in the back of our cavernous tin can on wheels while we sat up front, crowded together so we could hear what the others were saying.

For whatever reason, we were all in pretty introspective moods. Trent ended up being the ringleader for discussions that day, mostly over a book recommended by a friend who worked with him on the ropes course he managed during the summer. The friend in question – a younger guy named Nate who had a thing for climbing and Texas Hold 'Em – had been reading a book called *Blue Like Jazz* written by the somewhat disaffected evangelical writer Donald Miller. Its subtitle, "Nonreligious Thoughts on Christian Spirituality," gives you a clue that the book takes a hard and questioning look at what, for many people, was an established worldview of God, life and culture.

Trent devoured the book during those long hours on the road going over mountain passes and twisting our way down roads blasted into mountainsides. He'd pause occasionally to read aloud particular passages that caught his attention, kindling discussions from the group.

I got a copy of the book after I got home and found it pretty challenging. But at the same time, I could relate to this guy. He grew up in Texas, did the church youth group thing, but later found himself looking for something different. In his words, he wanted to go to the "green, lumpy places," which took him to Portland, Oregon, and to one of the most liberal of liberal arts schools, Reed College.

Miller found a home in a city that embraces its oddities. And he discovered a new facet of his spiritual journey (he writes about how he and some friends set up a "confessional booth" on campus for one particular event, but instead of people coming in to give confession, he and his friends would apologize to them for some of the hurtful excesses of the church. People weren't expecting that, and it turned out to be a hit).

So we found ourselves driving over narrow two-lane highways through our own green, lumpy places trying to see things from a different angle, particularly when it came to the ancient story of the flood from the Old Testament. Trent put it like this:

"As I read the book I began sharing excerpts from it with all of you. One in particular is still fresh in my mind. It was Miller's comparison of the 'perspective' of those contemporary to Noah with the 'perspective' we tend to find in typical Sunday School curriculums.

"While the writers of all those lessons emphasize the rescuing of the animal population and the survival of the human race and rainbows, the participants of the story experienced torrential rain, incredible flooding and death, and by inference…decay. Miller pointed out that our perception of a story or set of events can be significant to our view of truth."

Now there is a different take, but if you try, you can imagine it: Noah and his family in a shipload of animals. The odors of creatures and their waste waft through the stale, humid air inside. Incessant rain outside seeps in, compounding the feeling of damp, fetid rot. Beneath your feet, underneath the waves, is the destruction of the only world you ever knew. Though they were safely afloat, any promise of renewal seems far away in the midst of this watery cataclysm. It's definitely not the stuff of Sunday School nursery rhymes.

It would also be accurate to say that this view is not revisionist, only a different angle of the same story we all know. Through a different lens, the impact of the lesson changes, too.

"Reading this book was a significant jolt to my status quo," Trent said. "Previously, I perceived reality in a two-dimensional manner. As far as God was concerned, I was convinced that we were all looking at the same evidence, the same experiences, the same facts... I mean a fact is true whether I like it or not, right?

"What I found out on that trip is that we can all look at the same mountain, the same scripture, and the same relationships and see things completely differently."

And that's how we filled the spaces between destinations. We didn't talk much about Mount Elbert, the Black Canyon or fishing. We talked about life. We talked about the things of God, how we had come to see them, and the ways they might be perceived by others. Pretty deep stuff, and sometimes quite personal. Some of what was said in the van stayed in the van.

But it's no accident that for the group, the most memorable parts of the trip weren't the places we went, however spectacular they might be. What we recall most were the words spoken on winding Colorado roads, a time where good friends got to know each other on a deeper level.

It's hard to replicate that. Most people are dualities. There is the person everyone else knows: A carefully crafted persona of surface-level conversations, status updates, Instagram photos and other things designed to make us look beautiful, strong, adventurous, athletic, smart, holy or whatever. We build walls decorated with these ornaments of preferred imagery to make sure the public persona is all that anyone really knows, and that people gaze upon us approvingly.

But then there's our private side. This is the person who looks awful getting out of bed, picks his nose, sings badly in the shower or drinks too much. Anything from little quirks to major character flaws, tiny transgressions to serious sins. Only the sociopathic among us aren't affected by these shortcomings; the rest of us privately anguish over them while trying our hardest to make sure that no one knows what's behind the wizard's curtain.

You've made a real friend when you let someone witness the ugly inside, someone you allow to see the nasty bits, help you deal with them but respect you enough to not break the trust that such vulnerability implies. If you can befriend someone who will listen to what you really think (and not what we're all supposed to say), hear you out and not judge you, that's more valuable than gold.

That's what that group represented to me. We were able to reach that point on that trip, and in the years since, we've all seen those horrible, painful and at times ugly parts of our lives unfold and yet remain friends.

"This is where the 'who' of that trip matters most to me," Trent said. "The people who traveled with me did not try to 're-orient' me to the right or to the left. They participated in a trip within the trip with me. We shared our view of our destination with each other. We were all pilgrims. We were all traveling, but in the end, we all knew that our view of the trip would be incomplete if we were alone."

A group of friends in the midst of trying to live a little more adventurously, even if only for a few days, sometimes finds little treasures along the way that define the journey.

Maybe that ski trip was awesome. Perhaps your summit was so epic, so hard-earned and difficult and scary and exhilarating, that it became a defining moment of your life. But don't be surprised if it's something more subtle that captures your memories.

I never thought the best thing from that roadie back in 2005 was going to be found in a van traveling between Leadville and Gunnison, with giant peaks and deep canyons all around, talking about life through the prism of a paperback.

****

I'm amazed at the silliness I've been involved in on my many long drives. And grateful to God that I've survived them.

In college, while driving through the high plains with some buddies to go skiing, we once switched drivers while the car was still moving down the highway at seventy-five miles per hour. It was an awkward maneuver of one guy setting the cruise control, keeping a hand on the wheel while scooting to his right as I climbed over the bench seat from the back and clumsily slid into place to take over. Just dumb things college kids do, and usually we get away with it. I guess it doesn't matter that one wrong move in this little exchange could have made us all grease spots on the asphalt. But we lived through it and are now wiser through advanced years, having learned that such stupidity is not something to be repeated.

Thankfully, not all road trip foolishness is quite so dangerous.

A few years back, I was with a couple of friends, Ben and Kendra, my wife, Becca, and her sister, Liz, heading west to New Mexico. We planned to camp in the Carson National Forest and hike to the top of Wheeler Peak. Five of us were jammed into a late model Camry, streaking west across the same Oklahoma Panhandle highway I'd driven many times before. Suddenly Ben whipped the car to the side of the road and stopped. The door flew open, and he was on the run, sprinting through a muddy, recently cut cornfield.

Apparently, he'd seen a pheasant. Being an avid hunter, well, I guess his thirst for the blood of a game bird couldn't be contained.

We all had a good laugh. His shoes were caked with mud, and the pheasants were never in any real danger. Being in a crammed car for hours on end will make you do crazy things. And the absurdity of the moment is what made it perfect. I love Wheeler Peak and its many gorgeous vistas, but the pheasant chase is one of the recollections most seared into my brain from that particular trip.

Normal life is not usually filled with such random acts of frolic. The uninhibited glee over such a fruitless (yet oh so profitable) exercise like this marks the high point of any given road trip. Normal life can go days, weeks, or months without the mirth so generously provided on that drive. But these little roadies are often filled with memories that in some way shape us, flavoring our lives with something new, fun and unexpected.

A culinary metaphor might be something like this: Our mini adventures are like a wonderful bowl of pho, where you taste every flavor – the broth, noodles, meat, vegetables and spices – all at once. Most of the rest of our lives is like a bologna sandwich without even the benefit of a squirt of mustard.

Fun isn't the answer to all of life's problems, and I'm sure you can get by for a long time eating bologna sandwiches. But the rhetorical question is obvious: Would you really want to?

****

The trip was starting to wind down, with one more day to go before it was time to head home. We'd hiked all we'd planned to hike, fished where we wanted to fish, and were getting to the point where we were running out of time to cram in any more fun.

We still had to eat, though. We weren't too far from the west slope Colorado town of Montrose, a place big enough where we could get some cheap eats before settling down for the night. We wandered the town aimlessly. Indecision had set in.

"What sounds good?"

"I dunno. Anything I guess. What do you think?"

"I really don't care. Y'all decide."

And so it went for what seemed like an eternity but was actually just a few minutes. Time moves slowly when you're hungry and tired of being in a van. After a few rounds of that, we settled on a Wendy's.

We ambled in, road-weary and hungry and stepped up to the counter.

This was where the fun began.

The woman taking the order looked to be in her seventies. It appeared life had worked her over pretty good. She looked tired and not really wanting to be there. The details of our orders weren't easily conveyed. And she was lugging around an oxygen tank.

It took the four of us fifteen minutes to get our orders in. Not helping matters was the guy who was actually making the food.

If grandma at the counter had used up most of her life force by the time she'd ended up applying for this gig, the burnout cooking up the food was well on his way to lapping her. He looked to be in his twenties but was clearly not all there. He was slow, as in nothing he did translated into the pace you'd expect in a "fast food" joint. He wasn't particularly bright. No, let me rephrase that. He was dumb. Or maybe he was high.

Maybe both.

Much of the rest of the crew looked confused, untrained and not highly motivated.

It took awhile, but eventually the orders started coming in. All wrong.

A chicken sandwich ended up being a burger. A double burger was missing half the meat. And one other order that was completely jacked up.

But poor Jeff had the masterpiece of gastronomical ineptitude, one that stands the test of time.

Jeff had gone all out with his order, picking a bacon cheeseburger. It felt a bit light in the wrapper. As Jeff opened his little bundle of joy, its tragic contents revealed themselves.

Wilted lettuce.

Barely red tomatoes.

Two slices of "bacon" that looked like waterlogged, grease-stained strips of an old, gray paper bag rather than something that came from pork belly.

And no meat.

You read that right. A cheeseburger with no meat. Someone had carefully crafted this masterpiece with every component of the order (as sorry as they were), and wrapped that sucker up without bothering to check if the burger actually had a burger between the buns. It would be expected that you'd have a bunch of angry out-of-staters storm the counter and ream the poor souls who were running this asylum, but that's not what happened.

Instead, we all gathered around and gawked in awe at the spectacle before us. A cheeseburger with all the trimmings, minus the meat.

And Jeff just laughed.

Here's the thing. Jeff has one of those laughs, a high-pitched, gleeful thing, that's infectious. You can't help but to be happy when normally stoic Jeff bursts out with laughter. And that's what happened. The ensuing commentary was what you might expect to happen when a group of buddies gather for a retelling of a joke that still makes you chuckle. We got a lot of mileage out of that one, just making us laugh a little harder.

A few feet away, an employee was busily struggling with a mop, looking down at the floor, muttering to herself, "I just want to go home."

Tableau complete.

If the spirit of the long talks in the van defined this road trip, then the memory of the non-burger burger – and the highly improbable circus from which it came

– ended up being the signature moment. No summit view, no canyon panorama, none of that. I'm not sure anyone on that trip could recollect the precise details of what they saw from the top of Mount Elbert, but a decade after the Montrose Wendy's fiasco, all of us can remember Jeff's order, the crew that spawned it, and the forlorn mop-wielder who just wanted to call it a day.

This is the stuff that compels me to get on the road. Each element of this journey had some significance in that they all created a specific memory. But taken together they become much more potent. A lot happened in those five days when the four of us hit the road for Colorado: We summitted the highest peak in Colorado, hiked in one of the deepest canyons in the country, and caught numerous trout from cool, pristine waters. With a thought-provoking book as a catalyst, we gained a fuller understanding of who we were. And when we were well past the point of being road-weary, we got a much-needed laugh at our expense.

So I look back to what people say about adventure, that real adventure is dead. Maybe that's true by some stodgy explorer society's definition. For me, it's very much in your head. A good road trip has the elements of adventure in it. It's often a narrative of several individual experiences sewn together by a single goal, then spiced by unexpected events. It's accented by risk, success and failure. Joy and pain. Companionship or, in some cases, solitude. And often it is an event that has a lasting impact on you, be it for a season or a lifetime.

The days of Lewis and Clark or Hillary and Norgay may be far behind us, but that doesn't mean we shouldn't go looking for them just the same. We're lucky to have an open road that invites us to point that car in some direction, say "I'm going to go there" and then seek whatever lies around the bend.

I think Trent said it best when he described how, on another part of the trip, people were groaning about having to pay $12 for a burger at another mountain town. This was early on, when we'd just arrived. As the days piled up and the experiences mounted, perspectives changed. When the week ended and we returned home, something about us was different. Was it worth the time? The effort? The expense? I'd say so. I'm sure there are more luxurious ways to get away, but I doubt many of them would have had the same flavor.

When looking back at the end of the trip, Trent said, "Strangely, I don't recall any complaints about the cost of the burgers."

FOUR: TRAIL PEOPLE

"...(T)here is something about people you meet in the mountains and become friends with... Some people just become friends you feel secure with when hiking... you know they will stick with you, they keep you safe, know your strengths and weaknesses, and encourage you along the way."

– Noel Finta

Friends come quickly when you're a kid. There's an innocence about childhood where it's easier to trust your peers, and the medium on which friendships are built is usually as simple as the availability to come out and play. When you get older, friends might be people you meet in class, on your team, or in some other group where people find interesting or like-minded folks.

It gets more complicated as you age. Trust is harder to earn, but it's amazing how quickly people get together and become best buds in places like high school or college. In college, for example, you get a reset, where you go from knowing a bunch of people from your neighborhood or hometown to knowing almost no one, forcing you to crawl out of your protective shell, meet people and learn that a lot of them need a friendly face just as much as you.

I don't meet people easily. Every time I go to a new place or try to engage strangers in social functions, it doesn't feel right. It seems forced. Trust is a commodity I value highly, and I don't give it lightly. So I sit back, quietly observe, and maybe over time let folks in. It's not that I'm unfriendly or aloof, but I take my time cultivating relationships.

So imagine the potential discomfort with this scenario...

Step one: Get on social media and propose an idea to go on a trip into the mountains.

Step two: Get replies from strangers saying they'd like to be part of that plan.

Step three: Say, "OK, I'll go with you into a wild area without having any idea what spending hours in potentially uncomfortable places is going to be like with you."

On the surface, this sounds like a great way to get robbed or pushed off a cliff, depending on the intentions of the people you're meeting, or how weary of you they become after spending many hours with you in wild, uncomfortable places.

But here's the thing: I've done this before. I've done this a few times, and thus far, I have yet to regret any such meet-up to spend a day, or even several days, with folks I've never met.

This happens a lot among various outdoorsy communities. Climbers, hikers, backpackers, you get the drift. I like to call them trail people, because whatever it is they're doing, there is a decent chance it's going to include some time walking on a trail through the woods or in a desert or wherever.

Trail people are a different lot. Some of the finest people I know are men and women who I met, quite literally, at a trailhead, and thus far none of them have turned out to be stick-up artists or axe murderers. Their stories are often my stories, too, and because of that, those bonds of friendship seem to coalesce faster than they do in my non-trail world.

****

Sometimes you get to a point in life where you feel stuck. Whatever that might be, your Point A led to a Point B, and Point B didn't turn out to be what you'd hoped. Maybe it was radically different than what you expected, or a bit of a letdown. Point B can also be a gateway, a passage to change.

Point B eventually led my friend Chuck to Point C, which happened to be atop an icy, windblown summit on Colorado's Torreys Peak in the middle of winter. To hear him tell it, the journey to that summit was an eventful one, and one relying heavily on people who shared his growing fascination with the high country.

I've hiked with Chuck a few times, and climbed some of Colorado's highest with him. I find it almost impossible to keep up with the dude. He's built like a basketball small forward, long-legged and rangy, each stride seemingly consuming twice as much ground as mine. For a bigger guy, he moves smooth and fast, even at altitude. I think the last time I hiked with him I gave up keeping pace somewhere just past 11,000 feet. Staying on his heels was rather pointless for me, the hapless flatlander. I figured I'd see him later on, chilling on the summit, busting my chops when I arrived.

Chuck has climbed all of Colorado's 14,000-foot peaks, popularly known as the 14ers. His first peak was the same as it was for countless others, Grays Peak, a tall but relatively simple hike to its 14,270-foot summit, the highest spot in the Front Range. It's close to Denver, making it a popular destination for day hikers and people wanting to get their first 14er under their belt.

For Chuck, it was a date of sorts with a girlfriend well over a decade ago. They'd also hiked Mount Sniktau and a few other local peaks. That relationship passed, and it would be awhile longer before he'd hit the peaks again.

"After we broke up I never hiked again… instead, I dated, partied, got married (a second time), got fat, smoked, drank and just worked in the suburbia rat race," he said.

But Grays Peak planted a seed in his mind, and before long he was seeking advice from others about where to go and what to do in the high country. So he hit the gym, lost some weight, quit smoking and got online to learn more about the 14ers.

"I met some really cool people on the page (the 14ers.com website) and had a blast Facebooking with them. I was becoming obsessed with the fun that the 14er group page was becoming and needed to get back into climbing 14ers again. From mid-summer to October 2011, only after a few months in the gym and having quit ten years of smoking I hiked Quandary, Bierstadt, Sherman, Princeton, Shavano, and Antero," he said, ticking off the names of a few of those 14,000-foot peaks.

Like a lot of people, he obeyed the unwritten rules of when hiking season officially began and ended, assuming that things would be too cold, uncomfortable and dangerous when the snows began in the fall.

But then he saw some photos on that Facebook page of a woman getting her altitude fix on the flanks of Pikes Peak in the dead of winter. So he wrote her, asking questions, and built the confidence that maybe a winter summit isn't something reserved for hardcore mountaineers after all.

Chuck is a planner, so he kept doing the things he felt would give him the best chance of success in this coveted winter adventure. He kept hitting the gym, dropping down to a trim 195 pounds (down from north of 250 in his pre-14er life) and researched routes that were doable for a guy who had yet to challenge the peaks during winter. His work steered him back toward a familiar area, not far from his first 14er, Grays Peak. The plan: Drive to Loveland Pass, hike to Grizzly Peak, then traverse the distance between it and another one of the Front Range giants, Torreys Peak, Grays' slightly shorter but wilder sibling. He'd then hike down the Grays Peak trail into Stevens Gulch, where presumably a second car would be waiting and call it a day.

All he needed now were some companions.

He knew a guy named Durant, and they pulled in another dude from the virtual world, Rob. They followed a route along the Continental Divide, topping out on unnamed 12,000-foot peaks, then Cupid Peak, and later Grizzly Peak. From there, it was decision time, to see whether the conditions and their speed would allow them to continue on to Torreys' 14,267-foot summit. Once they dropped off Grizzly, they'd be committed to tackling Torreys and whatever the elements had in store, no small thing considering how quickly and dangerously conditions can change during a Rocky Mountain winter.

Fortunately, the weather cooperated. Unfortunately, gravity did not.

"From the top of Grizzly, Durant, Rob and myself had a quick rest to rehydrate and fuel up before finishing the first leg of the trip. Torreys lay in wait as we gathered our gear… well, as Durant and I gathered our gear. Rob had placed his new pack on the snow near the Grizzly summit and as we were all distracted milling through our packs for food and drink, Rob's pack began to slowly slide off the summit ridge, picked up momentum and was soon bounding down the slope and eventually veering off cliff edges and exploding with each airy bounce, jettisoning his food, drink and new gear he picked up just a day earlier, including his wife's cell phone. Luckily we had extra water and a few snacks that Rob would ration for the duration of the hike."

Safety is indeed found in numbers. Had Rob been alone, losing all that gear so far from a trailhead could have had dire consequences. Fortunately, his buddies had his back.

Eventually, the strain of the day caught up with Chuck. Fighting the snowpack, the winds, the steepness of the slope and the altitude made his legs heavy, and soon Durant and Rob began to fade out of sight. Chuck kept on, stopping to rest, adjust his pack or take in the views. As is often the case, weird and sometimes macabre thoughts crossed his mind.

"I actually thought about how long it would take Search and Rescue to come pick me up if I were to become too exhausted to continue."

He rallied, however, finding a rhythm and catching sight of his friends higher up. Waving his trekking poles to let them know he was still moving, he caught up and the three advanced to the top of Torreys Peak together.

Winter outings like Chuck's can be amazing because of the solitude. You and your group may be the only ones out there while everyone else is sequestered indoors or crowding ski lifts or doing something other than willing their way up the icy slopes of a high peak on a cold day. That was the case for Chuck, Durant and Rob, taking in sweeping views of nearby Front Range peaks, with even the giant mass of Pikes Peak visible from more than a hundred miles away.

That sort of solitude makes you feel special, as if what you see, hear and smell is there only for you – a reward for venturing out when others wouldn't, going places that are hard to get to and passing the physical and mental tests along the way. Using one of his trekking poles to steady his camera, Chuck began documenting the scenery in pictures.

Chuck's trip lasted a day, but the journey was much, much longer. When you live in Denver, you see the mountains every time you step outside and fix your gaze west. You wonder what it would be like to climb one. Mount Evans looms tall over the city, inviting you to come on up. And some do, like when Chuck and his ex-girlfriend did years ago, and perhaps that experience inspires more.

But as is often the case, getting to those places takes a team, with each person playing a specific role. You need an instigator to drag you out for a hike. You need an inspiration, a person doing things who makes you think, "Hey, if she can do it, why can't I?" And you need friends who can go with you, to be your safety net, your encouragement, your source of high-fives at the summit and people with whom you can retell stories over burgers and beer in some mountain town down the road from the trailhead, guys like Durant and Rob.

You need your trail people.

****

You might wonder how I came to know Chuck, or how I came to learn this part of his story. We didn't grow up together, we're not neighbors, and really, if not for a few chance encounters, I might never have met him at all. How I got to know Chuck was as simple as knowing someone who knew him, and having that guy respond to a call looking for people who might be interested in tackling a peak on a summer weekend when I happened to be in Denver.

That guy's name is Bill. Like many in the Colorado hiking scene, how I met Bill started with corresponding online, then later meeting face to face when I was hiking out from a backpacking trip in the San Juans.

Colorado's hiking community – its trail people – is dominated by those seeking the summits of the 14ers. There's an entire website dedicated to the 14ers, a comprehensive service with route descriptions, lists, real-time conditions reports and a forum for users to talk to each other about all things hiking, climbing and skiing the 14ers. One day a few years back I wrote a post on that forum about "Okie Mountaineering," describing some offseason climbing for people living in the Southern Plains. A gal named Beth had been doing some work in southeastern Oklahoma and messaged me about what hiking opportunities might be close to her job site.

We chatted about those topics for awhile, and then her brother joined in, her brother being Bill. I learned that they'd be hiking Uncompahgre Peak the same weekend I'd be there, but we all just missed each other until I was walking out on the four-wheel-drive road down the mountain. Bill and Beth were fortunate enough to have a rig that could handle the roughness of that road, and somehow they recognized me as they were easing their way down. Just like that, people in the virtual world met in the flesh.

We kept in touch over the years, and it was in preparing for a business trip to Denver that we got our first opportunity to hit the trail together. Bill answered my query by suggesting an alternative route up Torreys Peak.

Unlike that winter ascent of Torreys Peak that Chuck pursued, where no one was on the mountain except for him and his little group, Torreys Peak in the summer is a really busy place. Being so close to Denver and easy to get to, many people give it a try. Its most popular route is a hike – a strenuous one, for sure, but not something where any special skill or daring is required.

But Torreys Peak is somewhat complicated, with several other ways to the top. When snow is present, there is a deep, vertical gash down the middle of the mountain called Dead Dog Couloir that some people will try to climb, and for expert skiers, ride down. We wouldn't be doing that, but we would get a crack at a different path, that of scaling the peak from its wilder, more demanding Kelso Ridge.

Kelso Ridge is, at points, a steep line that includes several gullies and walls that take you from mere hiking to climbing. Many of these climbing spots overlook airy drop-offs some people can't stomach. One such wall overlooks Dead Dog, then tops out at the ridge's most dramatic feature, a short knife-edge ridge that abruptly ends at a large, white rock formation just below the summit. Going over that knife edge, then traversing the white rock is an exercise in absorbing the visuals of big air all around. If you're unduly scared of heights, I imagine this ridge would not be your idea of a good time. But if you can get past that, it really is a lot of fun to climb and it frees you from the conga line of day hikers trudging their way up the well-worn trail on the other side of the mountain.

This was the first time I'd been on a mountain with Bill and Beth. It was also the place where I first met Chuck, his friend Durant, and a cheery Colorado Springs hiker named Noel. You might remember how earlier I said that the prospect of online meet-ups is far outside of my comfort zone. And yet there I was, hanging out with a gaggle of new friends on a mountain, enjoying a spectacular, blue-bird day after tackling what was, for me at the time, a challenging line to the top. Kelso Ridge may have been the first time I'd hiked with this bunch, but it would not be the last.

To hear Bill tell it, his story is not much different.

Bill had done some hiking earlier in life, but it was Beth that got him into doing the 14ers. She was talking about going up Huron Peak, a gorgeous hike with some of the most dramatic views in the entire Sawatch Range of central Colorado. Bill's interest was piqued.

"I distinctly remember one July morning in 2002, when my sister, who had been climbing some 14ers in the past, had said that she was planning on climbing Huron Peak. Something inside me just leaped out and asked if I could come," he said.

So on August 2 of that year (the date is seared into his memory), Bill summitted Huron Peak, his first 14er, and a new passion was born. He got a few more under his belt and formed a group called "The Lardass 14ers Club" ("We had T-shirts made," he notes). Beth served as Bill's guide for awhile, and as the group grew and he got to know more like-minded people, an entirely new circle of friends was found. Many years and many peaks later, I became a small part of that growing crowd.

During a more recent summer outing into the San Juans, Bill was driving a group of us around and we were discussing the type of people who like exploring the mountains. He had a friend of his, a young gal named Jenny, and I'd brought a buddy from Tulsa, Matt, who was looking to climb his first 14er. As a matter of passing time, I asked Bill and Jenny what it was about their "mountain" friends that made them different from others. Bill had some good insight on this subject, and he held court as he drove Jenny's Nissan Pathfinder down the road.

He separated it into a couple of categories. First was how the 14er community relates as a group. And the second, how people in the community relate to one another individually.

He likened the group dynamic to that of a high school. Not in the way that high schools divide up into interests or cliques or whatever, but in simpler terms, how it organizes by grade levels, and in turn, how those grades interact. It's the same deal with the 14ers crowd, with wide-eyed newbies trying their best to fit in and learn from experienced mountaineers by way of listening to their stories, asking questions and hoping to tag along on the next adventure.

I found that take rather fascinating. I guess I'd never thought about it that way, but the more I explored the idea, the more it made sense. I'd unwittingly become an underclassman at 14er High and was just now figuring that out. Remembering that conversation, we revisited it later on so he could elaborate.

"You first get there, and everyone who is already there looks older and more impressive, even if they aren't... the simple fact that they were there before you makes them knowledgeable and experienced," Bill said. "As you first start to talk, you find people who are similar in skill level and need (AKA the same grade as you) so you make plans with these guys knowing that the logistics of climbing will be similar in this group."

To further the analogy, 14er High has a subset, a dating scene that is alarmingly similar to what we all saw and experienced while walking down the halls at school. Guys and gals find their love of the peaks leads to a flirt, a date, a hook-up and probably a peak or five. But, as Bill warns, it has its pitfalls: "Like high school, that group of people is sometimes catty, full of drama and gossip."

It's an interesting mix, to say the least, fueled by meet-ups at Denver or Colorado Springs bars. Fourteener Happy Hours are where the whole student body can get together, have a few drinks, tell tall tales, dish dirt, meet girls/guys and scheme for that next big mountain trip.

The group also plans "gatherings," where a spot is selected in which to camp, and anyone who wants to come is invited. Fall, spring and winter gatherings allow people floating in the ether to meet up on the trail and hike or climb with the rest of the community. It's different than the happy hours because there is actual hiking going on, but a lot of the other elements of those happy hours, both good and bad, are the same.

In any case, these are the ways this particular outdoor community bonds. Instead of doing it at house parties, football games or class trips, they coalesce around the peaks. But time passes, and just like high school, the nature of the people changes as well. Beginners start bagging more summits, and before long they have dozens of peaks to their credit and all the requisite scars, wisdom and memories that come with them.

"As you grow through the seasons, you increase in class – sophomores, juniors, seniors. It's all the same," Bill said. "You start to become the elders that 'newbies' look up to, who think you are the most experienced person, or people, they've ever seen. In reality, I am nothing like that, but try convincing some of these folks of that. So, as you either finish the 14ers, or they lose a relevancy in your life, you have 'graduated.' You may not hang around as much anymore. If you attend happy hours or the gatherings you are looked at by some like the high school kids look at the college kids who come back to the high school parties... 'Who is this old timer, is he just going to talk about climbing in his day?' Sooner or later you stop going to happy hours as you cannot relate to the new crop of climbers."

Of course, that is just one facet, one rough analogy, of how trail folk relate. It's a good one, as it explains quite a bit. But there is more to the story.

Among other things, the mountains are places that fuel ambition, and right or wrong, self-worth. On a more basic level, they are sources of adrenaline, as the nature of mountains – that of being big, wild, and at times, dangerous – makes them scenes of high intensity. The sense of achievement over tackling a difficult climb can be a serious high, just like a close brush with death. Memories associated with the darker side of the mountain experience – the loss of a friend, or perhaps a debilitating accident – can bring you down just as low as those successful summits can lift you up. Fear is a common element in all this, like a storm cloud bubbling with dark, angry potency, power and foreboding, where overcoming it makes you feel like a dragon slayer while succumbing to it is akin to being run out of your own home. You can come back from a simple day hike with strangers and feel friendly toward them, but when you get off a mountain with any or all of the experiences I just related, something else happens entirely. A bond will be created that is not easily explained. It's safe to say that intense experiences lead to intense feelings and leave it at that.

This creates a peculiar dynamic among those who share these moments of risk. Friendships come fast: They run hot, but they have their limitations. What do you have in common outside of the mountains? If you can't answer that question with anything of substance, you might never see a lot of the friends you made on the trail if you or they, for whatever reason, leave that part of life behind to make room for other things. And those romances? It's the same deal, but turbocharged, shining bright for a time, then burning out if the couple in question don't have anything else holding them together aside from their love of the outdoors.

Bill has experienced all of that.

"When you are climbing in a group of friends, and climbing a lot – you develop a friendship based on trust abnormally quick," he said. "Same with the girlfriends. You sort of fall in love real quick, because while no one admits what they are doing on the peaks is very dangerous – you are in a precarious place with that person or those people – you can't help but over-inflate some feelings for these people up front.

Not saying it's fake friendships. But it's rushed, and that's natural. As soon as the intensity is over, people mostly go their separate ways looking for their next fix, whatever that is."

Still, it's not uncommon for those bonds to endure. In our subsequent conversations, Bill mentioned to me a group of friends who became known as "the brat pack," climbers who were all in the same stages of experience and ambition who were cemented even further by the death of a friend, mountaineer Rob Jansen, who was killed in a freak rockslide on Hagerman Peak in 2012. His death hit them hard, making them all the more determined to climb the peaks in a way that would make their fallen friend proud.

"I think many people have a core group in friendships, and something distinctly defines that core group. For us, the loss of Rob Jansen defined us. We were determined, and successful, in finishing the 14ers for us, for him."

Bill acknowledged that the brat pack is not as active as it once was. But given the chance, he'd gear up with them again.

"I consider every person I've hiked with a kindred spirit, and someone I'd definitely consider a friend if asked. But it's like everything in life, as we grow and develop more interests elsewhere, you change the scene. They always stay a part of your past, perhaps a couple will become lifelong friends.

"I still talk to all of the others and will climb with any of them in a second if asked."

****

It's funny how the things Bill described have manifested themselves in my own behavior. A few months after we topped out on Torreys Peak, Bill was getting ready to summit the final Colorado 14er on his list, Mount of the Holy Cross, a gorgeous sentinel in the northern Sawatch Range not far from Vail. A friend of his was also finishing up on Holy Cross, so the party was going to be big. A couple of dozen people drove to the tiny town of Minturn, then weaved up a lonely dirt road to a campsite a few more miles away.

I joined that group. I had no time off from work, so if I wanted to be there, I'd have to drive from Tulsa to Minturn (and the campsite), get up the next morning to climb the peak, head back down and drive home, all within the space of three days, thirty hours of which was spent driving. It was a stupid plan, but the draw was being able to be there for Bill and meet up with the gang I'd met on Kelso Ridge. It was a tremendous expense of time and energy for a fella I'd seen three times in my life, but at the time it seemed totally worth it.

I got back to Tulsa with maybe a few hours of sleep between the time I left to the time I returned, and still worked a full shift. I'm not sure I've ever been that tired, despite the volumes of Mountain Dews and Five-Hour Energy drinks I consumed. It was a foolish thing to do, and not something to be repeated, but I have zero regrets about it.

But why? Why go through such great lengths to get in one more mountain trip? Maybe it was a sense of kinship with the people on that mountain. There were possibilities there beyond the potential for new adventures, something closer to finding a level of authenticity lacking elsewhere in my life. Maybe that was an illusion, caused by what Bill described as an inflated bond produced by the rush of the climb. Even with that in mind, I felt there was more out there.

I got a similar sense from Noel, or at least from her story.

Noel is an Air Force veteran who had settled into family life in Colorado Springs. She devoted much of her adult life to raising her kids, adding a little fun via her creative and prolific baking streak. But over time the kids grew up, moved out and started lives of their own. A void was created, a blank spot ultimately filled when she was cleaning out a closet and found a pair of her son's childhood hiking boots. They were still in great shape and looked like they might fit.

So she tried them on. Lo and behold, like the glass slipper from Cinderella fame, they were just her size.

Noel found her way to the slopes of Pikes Peak, that monster mountain looming over the Springs, and its popular Barr Trail. The more she hiked, the stronger she got, and suddenly a new chapter in her life unfolded. A friendly sort, Noel would tote small containers of homemade cookies in her pack, offering her goodies to people she hiked with and even strangers she met on the trail. Finding those boots, walking up the Barr Trail, and topping out on Pikes Peak, a new Noel was born.

She became the Cookie Hiker.

She made a lot of friends on the trail, and discovered something different in the 14er community than what existed elsewhere in her life, a drive and commitment among these hikers and mountaineers that she found admirable.

"These friends have that extra level of understanding of what it takes to climb some of these mountains that my non-hiking friends will just never really be able to grasp," Noel told me. "There is a bond there with these friends because they know the skill, attention, physical training, and mental toughness it takes to do some of these climbs. They understand the passion of the sometimes-risky sport of mountain climbing and are as thrilled to talk about it as I am. Trying to explain these things to others doesn't always compute with them.

"Overall, in just five years of hiking, I have made more friends than I have in many years when I led a non-hiking life."

Noel has evolved over the years, adding skills to her tool box that include things like sport climbing, trad climbing and even ice climbing. She regularly hikes up Pikes Peak's mellower trails, but included in her ascents are some of the toughest in all of Colorado. Most recently, she and two friends climbed Mount Rainier, the biggest and burliest of the Cascades of Washington state.

Tackling those harder peaks has also given her perspective on trust and teamwork, not to mention a healthy regard for the dangers these mountains present.

Anyone who has been up in the mountains very often can probably tell you about close calls. Many times, it's a story involving a quick change in the weather, or perhaps a near fall. Illness can also come into play. Most ascents are incident-free, but the mountains aren't designed by risk managers or lawyers and there aren't any handrails up there. Sometimes bad things happen.

A few years back, Noel came face to face with that. She was with a group climbing one of Colorado's hardest and most intimidating mountains, Capitol Peak. It's the baddest of the bad boys in the Elk Range, a line of mountains known for their extreme beauty, dramatic profiles and potential for danger. The Maroon Bells are nicknamed "the Deadly Bells" because of the fatal encounters that have transpired there. Across the valley from the Bells, Pyramid Peak shares their more unsavory attributes – it's steep, exposed, and littered with loose rock that only heightens the risk of falls and rockslides. Snowmass Mountain, in the words of people I know, "moves beneath your feet."

But Capitol Peak seems to be a whole other animal. It's remote, making it a bit of a haul to get to its lower flanks. The easiest way up includes a hike up its steep shoulder, then climbing over or around a prominent feature on its ridgeline called "K2," which can be dicey – the scramble is a steep one, and the drop-offs on either side are significant. Once you get past K2, Capitol's signature feature awaits – a long, slender and ridiculously exposed knife-edge ridge that takes a bit of nerve to traverse. The rock is said to be quite solid, but this is a place where you cannot move fast, cannot be careless and absolutely cannot afford a misstep. The knife-edge ridge is a "no-fall zone," meaning that if you fall here, the certainty of death is pretty much one-hundred percent.

When you get past the ridge and take on Capitol's summit pitch, the peak reveals itself to be kin to its Elk Range neighbors – steep, complicated, and plagued with crumbling, rotten rock.

By the summer of 2013, Noel had honed her mountaineering skills to the point where an attempt at Capitol was realistic. So she joined a group of friends to climb it and hopefully add another notch to an impressively growing collection of high country accomplishments.

The hike up to K2 went fine, as did the knife-edge ridge traverse. Near the top of the mountain, however, things went awry.

From above, a rock moved, then tumbled down toward her. She got a warning, but not before the toaster-sized stone crashed on top of her helmeted head. A second rock trailed behind, smashing into the side of her skull. One of the rocks also struck her left forearm, causing immediate swelling. She thought it might have been broken, but the contusion didn't limit her mobility. In true Noel fashion, she wrapped up her arm, dusted off, and finished the climb.

The bad stuff happened after. She didn't realize it until later, when they were off the mountain, but the rocks that struck her in the head caused a severe concussion that for a time looked as though it might alter her life for good. Subsequent doctor visits showed significant brain trauma that somehow didn't manifest itself until after she'd gotten down. The helmet likely saved her life, but it couldn't undo the consequences of the rockfall impact.

Caring for her injured arm, finishing the climb and then getting back down proved to be important in other ways, too. Anyone who hears her story marvels at how she completed the climb at all, considering what had happened to her and the difficulties that descending the peak still had in store. But the way that her climbing partners were able to administer first-aid, encourage her to the summit, and be there during the descent made an impression. After Capitol Peak, these weren't just people who shared some good memories. They were, more than most, people she could trust with her safety, even her life. She'd circle back to these climbers again for future challenges.

The following year was not an easy one for Noel. Battling "brain pain" on a daily basis was (and still is) a grinding exercise of forbearance, exhausting in its seemingly untiring persistence. Noel is a cheerful sort and not given to complaining about her troubles, but as is often the case with people suffering from chronic and debilitating pain, the struggle wears on you. Most people don't know how much you suffer and can't really understand it. But in her own trail community, she found the support and encouragement she needed – that it was possible to suffer these pains and still keep doing the things you love. An understanding voice – as well as a chorus of well-wishers offering encouragement where they could – helped her get through some of the darkest times following the rockfall incident on Capitol Peak. The thing all these people had in common is they were folks she'd gotten to know in the days and years after she first set foot on the Barr Trail in her kid's old hiking boots.

Nearly a year later, a group of us gathered to climb Wetterhorn Peak, a gorgeous precipice in southwestern Colorado that would be the first somewhat challenging mountain Noel had attempted since the Capitol climb. Wetterhorn turned Noel back the last time she was there – dicey snow conditions just below the summit and right above some sizable cliffs made the risks feel too great – making it her "nemesis" peak. Given those circumstances, this particular trip had the potential to be emotionally charged.

The hike up the mountain's shoulder went well, and we took a quick pause before trudging up the "yellow dirt" portion of the ridge just before the rockier, tougher sections of the mountain. Noel welled up with emotions for a bit, collected herself, and then blasted up the hill until she stood on the chunky, sun-cupped snow on Wetterhorn's airy summit. She'd done plenty of tougher peaks before, but the significance here – tackling the only mountain to have previously turned her away, and moving past the mental barriers that often follow physical trauma – made this summit particularly significant.

But to hear her tell it, it's the people she was with who made the day, and continue to be a major part of why she enjoys these adventures so much. High-fives and hugs were shared all around. As well as some cookies.

"I have a select few friends I hike with often, because I know we complement one another's hiking abilities and I enjoy their company very much," she said. "There have been some friends who instantly click with me and I know we will remain lifelong friends from our experiences in the mountains. Just to have someone truly understand and explain how things are going to be and encourage me along in my journey means the world to me and helps me get through."

****

I've spent much of my life doing outdoorsy things, with a good chunk of that on trails, hiking to fishing holes or setting up campsites in the backcountry. We'd build fires, sometimes far too big to be safe, sometimes just big enough to give everyone that nice, warm glow that can only emanate from the small, flickering flames dancing within the tight confines of a fire ring. But it's only been for the last dozen years I've been taking these adventures to high mountain summits, first with friends from home, and eventually, with people I'd meet along the way.

These are definitely two different categories of people. I know a lot of people from work, church, high school or college or whatever, and how we came to know one another varies in more ways than I can recollect. But the second group is different in that how I met them (never mind the medium) is pretty consistent. Had it not been for a shared love of the high country, I'd never have known Chuck, Bill or Noel, or a whole host of others. But because of the mountains I know who they are, and on the trail is where I've learned more about their lives.

I stopped one night to contemplate this, to get a partial tally of the different folks I've met, people with whom I've hiked, camped and climbed. A sampling:

There's an architect and an interior designer.

Air Force vets and a combat soldier.

A weed dealer and an air traffic controller.

An accountant and a ski bum.

A bar tender, a physical therapist and a musician.

And a supercharged, super-tatted vegan/ridge runner/engineering student who wants to change the world.

I know Chuck could probably make a good living as a photographer, I know how to get to Bill's house and the name of his dog, and I know the nicknames Noel has given her grandkids. All because we love the mountains and were willing to take a chance at spending time with people who were complete strangers at a trailhead and came back from the summit as friends.

Shared passions are important here, but I think Noel had it right: It's the shared experiences on the trail that sealed the deal.

You could call us a tribe, a trail people tribe. Folks who aren't born into a lineage, but rather bound by an appreciation of shared victories and an understanding of common struggles. It's not an easy thing to understand unless you've been there, working out the soreness of a long backpacking stretch, being breathless on a high peak, or facing down looming fears. Those experiences become a part of you, just like the people with whom you've shared them.

FIVE: GOING SOLO

"It had nothing to do with gear or footwear or the backpacking fads or philosophies of any particular era or even with getting from point A to point B.

"It had to do with how it felt to be in the wild. With what it was like to walk for miles with no reason other than to witness the accumulation of trees and meadows, mountains and deserts, streams and rocks, rivers and grasses, sunrises and sunsets. The experience was powerful and fundamental. It seemed to me that it had always felt like this to be a human in the wild, and as long as the wild existed it would always feel this way." — Cheryl Strayed

The first time I read one of those Huffington Post articles about "what every introvert wants you to know," I could relate. I veer toward the introverted direction. But by the time that article had spun around social media circles about forty times, or shortly after Buzzfeed and every other new media clickbait factory had written their own version of it, I'd had my fill. I mean, please. Enough of the angsty introvert crap. We get it already. I guess there is a huge market for folks who don't like being around people and want everyone to know about it.

I like people. I like being around people. Not all the time, and certainly not talking on the phone. But if I get away from people for too long I get horrifically unproductive, lazy and lumpish. The right people can be motivating, energizing forces. So I'm not good for the hermit thing. I might be an introvert to some degree, but I'm not antisocial. I need the fellowship of other human beings.

One of the down sides of being around people, however, is the noise. Yes, there is the actual, audible noise, but this also includes the "noise" of things that come with people these days: screaming Facebook posts during election season; a ceaseless parade of silly cat videos; the torrential deluge of car/gym/bathroom selfies; inane newscasts and pundit programs that make the nation a little dumber every day. These count as noise, and after awhile we become so oversaturated with the racket it gets to the point of neurosis.

I've got a reservoir of sorts. It's a big one, but it has its limits. It's my noise reservoir. Once that big ole tank gets full, I have to empty it.

Sometimes going out for a run does the trick, especially if it's a run on the trails. Trail runs are awesome for emptying noise reservoirs. Thus far, however, my longest trail runs (in terms of duration) are six hours or less. So while they help keep the noise tank from overflowing, it's a temporary fix that can be overwhelmed if I encounter a little too much stupid back in the world of people. When I get to that point, a more drastic reboot is needed.

How I get that might be a little different than a lot of people. A pub crawl or a weekend of Netflix doesn't do it for me. One hurts my head and the other just turns me into a slug. Feeling awful doesn't help.

What does help? Understanding who I am, for starters. I'm a social person, but I'm also very much someone who is comfortable with long periods of solitude. That really helps if you're a writer, and it's also useful if you're into long-distance running. Check and check.

But what's also needed is quiet. Real quiet.

I find quiet places in wilderness, and when it comes to emptying the noise reservoir, this is something that needs to happen when I'm alone. While we're at it, let's make that alone time something that lasts for at least a couple of days. Most of the time, I'd rather enjoy a summit view or a beautiful hike with friends. But there is a particular satisfaction – maybe even joy – that comes with earning that view with no one else around with whom to celebrate.

The process, however, can be an ordeal most normal people won't stomach. Obviously, it can be lonely. In some ways, it can be scary. Can it be boring? That's possible. But it's part of the process for people like me. People like me need to be alone sometimes.

Really, really alone.

****

I'm different than my peers, especially where I live in the Southern Plains. I wasn't athletically minded when I was a kid, though a lot of the seeds of sports and the outdoors planted back then still stick today. But how this has influenced me is not the same as it is for most dudes I know.

It's hard to explain in an elegant way. I like the way Jim Rome does it better. He's one of the biggest names in sports talk radio, mostly because of the biting humor he throws out there every day. That's probably why I like him.

He talks about caricature figures, like Fantasy Football Guy or Rec League Softball Guy. These are my favorite Jim Rome bits, and it got me to thinking about a few of them in my own world. So with apologies to Mr. Rome, let me elaborate.

Rec League Softball Guy loves sports. He probably used to play some baseball, and age has made it more convenient to play a baseball-like game with a bigger ball thrown slowly underhand toward the plate. Rec

League Softball Guy does not have to be athletic or even in shape to play and play well. But Rec League Softball Guy takes his game seriously, even to the point of arguing balls and strikes, or other calls an umpire might make. Rec League Softball Guy might even start fights during games. I give credit to Rec League Softball Guy for getting outside and moving, but deduct points for the grave importance slow-pitch softball seems to have in his life.

I tried to be Rec League Softball Guy, but I don't throw accurately, don't hit well, can't field the ball worth a darn, and just don't care enough to be part of the club. I haven't picked up a bat, ball and glove in 15 years.

There's also the Golf Potato. Golfers tend to come in a couple of varieties. Really good golfers will play well enough to qualify for pro-am events, and they walk the course. The Golf Potato might come close, but he rides the cart. Golf Potatoes hang artwork in their homes and offices depicting beautiful greens on famous golf courses from around the world, and they own more golf shirts than they do any other kind of clothing. They'll spend wads of cash on clubs, balls, bags and other gear and will actually watch entire PGA telecasts and like it.

I tried to be a Golf Potato. Golf is a good time. You get to spend hours outside, and if you don't take the game seriously (I don't, because I suck) it's a fantastic way to spend the day. But I can't afford the lifestyle. I don't play enough to get better, I have to rent or borrow clubs, and I frustrate fellow golfers who are actually good (though my nephew Jordan is wonderfully patient and fun to play with). But if I'm going to spend a few hours outside, I'd rather it be hiking, or hitting a summit, or torturing my body running hilly trails. It's warped thinking to most people, and completely vexing to Golf Potatoes. We visit each other's universes, but happily return to our own when it's done.

Then you've got the Yard Nerd. These guys are mostly a suburban breed, driven to great lengths to green up their lawns and create landscaping on their private slice of heaven so ornate and manicured that you'd think they had professional assistance to get it done. Some of their neighbors seek hired help to compete with the Yard Nerd, but they are not his equal, mostly because they don't spend the time and effort Yard Nerd does in actually doing the work. Yard Nerd fertilizes his own yard. He treats that yard for weeds and pests. He routinely mows, trims, edges and prunes. His garage is a vault of garden and lawn tools, and the really dedicated Yard Nerds don't push a mower. They ride one. The size of the yard doesn't matter. A small lot can still be mowed with your butt planted on a small tractor with a mowing deck, as I've seen numerous times.

I tried (half-heartedly) to be a Yard Nerd. But I can't stand mowing. Or trimming. Or edging. Or pruning. All the upkeep that comes with nurturing flowers and eradicating weeds, plus all that other work, led me to believe there comes a point where the yard simply exists to keep Yard Nerd busy, which seems to be the opposite of why you'd want to have a yard in the first place, that is, to *enjoy* your outdoor space. I give credit to Yard Nerd for getting outside, getting dirty and not mailing it in on the couch. But if I'm going to spend time outdoors, well, see my reasons above for not being a Golf Potato.

Closely related to Yard Nerd is Home Improvement Guy. This is the person who, along with the rest of his tribe, keeps places like Home Depot, Lowe's and ACE Hardware in business. Home Improvement Guy is different than a contractor or carpenter in that remodeling his home, or working on fixer-uppers, is not his vocation. It's his hobby. Like Yard Nerd, his garage is a vault of sorts, but his treasures include tools most trim carpenters would envy. Home Improvement Guy can lay tile, install a tub, put up a ceiling fan, and work power tools like a boss. I totally love the idea of being proficient with such tools, and I can work a few of them. My first job in high school was as a general laborer for a construction company, and I'm good at digging holes, lifting things and working sheetrock. But again, all that time and money remodeling a kitchen could get me weeks of backpacking, trail running and mountaineering.

I guess it's no surprise that for several years I rented an urban apartment where yards and home improvement were someone else's job.

Lastly, there's Gun Guy. Now this one is a little trickier to define, as lots of people in this country own guns. I own guns. But Gun Guy is different than the occasional hunter or someone who buys a pistol for self-protection or sport. These folks have their reasons for owning a gun, but they aren't Gun Guy.

Gun Guy likes guns. I mean, REALLY likes guns. Gun Guy owns lots of guns. Handguns. Shotguns. Hunting rifles. Assault rifles. But just be sure not to tell Gun Guy that his AR-15 or AK-47 is an assault rifle or you'll get a lecture on political correctness, the Second Amendment and freedom. Gun Guy posts lots of memes on social media about guns. The more hardcore Gun Guy believes that he and folks like him are a major part of keeping America safe from tyrants, terrorists and liberals. Gun Guy will spend thousands of dollars on more guns, and his gun safe is a lot like the garage of Yard Nerd and Home Improvement Guy in that this is where his treasure lies.

I don't think I've ever tried to be Gun Guy, though I have dabbled in Gun Guy's world. Like I said, I own guns. Two of them. At one time, my arsenal included two 12-gauge shotguns and a .22-caliber semiautomatic rifle with a scope, which sounds a lot more sinister to the uninitiated until you see it. It's more like the first gun you buy junior for plinking targets or pasture pests. Anyway, I've shot all these plus a whole variety of handguns and rifles, including those reviled/revered AR-15s and AK-47s. I won't lie, shooting guns is fun. Hunting can be a great way to spend time outside, and there's something pretty boss about being able to go out into the woods and bring back dinner. I support people's right to defend themselves with firearms, and I'm not freaked out when I see some dude doing the open-carry thing.

But I'm under no illusion that me and my two shotguns (I sold the .22 a long time ago) are a bulwark against a totalitarian takeover, and frankly, neither are the legions of Gun Guys with their sizable weapons stashes. I haven't been hunting in years, I can't shoot skeet worth a damn and get bored easily when the discussions drift toward gun-talk. Most Gun Guys own way more weapons than they need, and most people who choose to build these huge collections and carry sidearms openly are technically exercising their rights, but are really doing what they do as some sort of expression of masculine power.

Every guy wants to be seen as a potential warrior figure, a mighty hero that could easily be the fella yelling "Wolverines!" when the commies come to town, but let's face it – the modern American world is mostly devoid of the dangers seen in the Dark Ages, and with the absence of such perils, some folks need to find an outlet to become the fighter in their mind that they'll likely never be in reality. Looking/feeling dangerous will have to do.

I can see where some people would be offended by these characterizations. Stereotyping can seem a little mean-spirited, but I do this in good fun. We must be able to laugh at ourselves, because in some way we're all a little ridiculous. In the same way that the passions of the people I've listed above leave me a little bored, my dronings about mountains, trails, long runs and big hikes don't go long without eliciting yawns from folks who just aren't that into it.

Similarly, the treasure troves of softball gear/trophies, golf gear/wardrobes, gun stashes, power tools and lawn equipment aren't a lot different from my own hoard of tents, backpacks, hiking boots, trekking poles, camp stoves, sleeping bags, running shoes and tech shirts. The adoration Gun Guy has for his laser-sighted AR or Golf Potato's sparkling set of Callaways is no more intense than my love for my crampons, ice axe or trail runners.

Everyone has an inner nerd ready to geek out on something, and that's totally OK. My trouble is I'm badly outnumbered by Rec League Softball Guys, Golf Potatoes, Yard Nerds, Home Improvement Guys and Gun Guys. That means I get left out of a lot of conversations.

So more often than not, I run alone. Sometimes I hike alone. Or even climb alone. I guess that suits me. I like people just fine, but I don't mind the solitude. I'm used to playing the role of the outsider.

****

I don't want to get into how badly we have devolved into beings who must be constantly busy, how the TV is always on, or how our eyes are always pointed down toward our phones or tablets or whatever electronic doodad snags us in its virtual snare. That topic has been broached often enough, with the general consensus being that it's bad for us. For the most part, I agree.

It all goes back to that noise I was talking about, and how for most of us, we never get a break from it. Not anymore. Long periods of quiet, or solitude, are rare.

It's in that respect I pity millennials. They haven't lived in the days before the Internet, or before the time when mobile phones and other smart devices became ubiquitous. The rest of us have. Most of us know what it's like to experience long stretches of solitude. It was easier to empty the reservoir back then than it is now. It's always been an intentional act to achieve solitude, so I'm grateful I've had plenty of practice.

Back when I was in college, my family was spread out all over the world. At one point, I had a sister in west Texas, a brother in Colorado, another brother in Germany and my parents in France. I was taking courses at a small Baptist liberal arts college smack in the middle of Oklahoma.

It was cool being on my own. I liked school. I had good friends, things to do and a certain feeling of, dare I say, "accomplishment" for making it on my own. Never mind that I had my parents' gas card and plenty of help along the way. But I digress.

When the holidays rolled around and the campus cleared out, I'd sometimes make my way to my sister's place in Midland, a small west Texas city built on the petro-riches found deep underground in the Permian Basin. The routine: Load up my duffle, slip on a thick hoodie and a faded denim jacket, and buy a pack of cheap cigars. Then I'd start up my truck, slip it into gear and roll southwest to the flattest land in all of Texas. That's an eight-hour drive, boring as hell and I loved every minute of it.

This may not sound like your idea of a good time, but hear me out. After a semester of communal living, tight class schedules, high stress and all that other business, those eight hours on the road — blowing cigar smoke out the window as the soundtrack of the engine, the tires on the road and the music on the radio droned on — were just the release I needed. The yellow, orange, red and purple glow of the sun setting over the horizon was a pretty sweet bonus.

I'm sure the trip would have gone by faster with some company, but then I wouldn't have been able to burn all those cigars, wouldn't have been able to sing all those songs at full volume, and wouldn't have had all that time to decompress.

Going solo is often about just that – decompression. The time alone without distractions to drink in what's going on around you without having to satisfy anyone else's agenda but your own is exactly the tonic I need when life gets a little too crazy.

I had a couple of years not long ago when life was really going awry. In the middle of all that, I also got to enjoy one of the most amazing and memorable outdoor experiences of my life. A solo hike in the Wichita Mountains of southwestern Oklahoma included a near-miss with an angry buffalo, a record-setting torrential rain storm and some absolutely incredible scenery (more on that later).

When I tell people about that hike, they wonder aloud what would have happened to me if that buffalo had gored me (self-rescue would have been a serious issue), or how I could possibly enjoy being soaked to the bone for hours on end.

But being alone allowed me to really pay attention to my surroundings. When you're solo, your senses are heightened to a point where every sight, smell and scent is far more intense than if you had shared it with others.

It also gave me time to think. And believe me, I had a lot on my mind.

Focusing on the task at hand – navigating wilderness with no one else there to help – allowed me to escape. Maybe not forget. But even if for a day or two, just to not be where all the world's troubles were, where all my problems were – yes, that is an escape. As hostile as the conditions and maybe the wildlife were, that place at that time was a refuge not unlike the smoke-filled cab of my little pickup motoring down a west Texas highway, with The Eagles blaring from the speakers and not a care to be had.

There is solace in the toil of journeying alone.

****

Call it a hangup from junior high and high school, but most people aren't comfortable going to a public place, like a restaurant, and eating alone. How many people do you know who intentionally go out to eat solo? Not many, I'll bet. Maybe none.

The same goes for movies. There are a few, sure, but for the most part folks see movies with other people.

Having a drink at a bar while solo is also pretty novel. So much so that it appeared on some trendy website's list of things to do before you die. Really? Drinking alone at a bar is now a bucket list thing? Maybe it is if your intent is not to meet someone, but rather just sit there at the bar, order a bourbon, and sip that bad boy while silently observing bar behavior. I'll bet it could be fascinating, but also a little creepy.

But if you're totally at ease with any or all of these activities while alone, you're a rare bird. It takes a degree of self-confidence to march solo into an establishment that is social in nature, do your business, and leave without regard to what anyone else thinks.

Confidence is also a valuable commodity when going it alone in wild places. You can trust me on this one – if you walk into the woods, or the desert, or some other wilderness environment with no one but *you* to count on, that confidence will be tested, and not just by the environment in which you are entering. It will be tested by your mind.

When you're with someone, or with lots of people, there is always an opportunity for feedback. If someone needs help, other hands are available. There is safety in numbers, safety from dangers both real and perceived. When the task at hand is particularly difficult, other people can be a source of encouragement.

Now take all of that away, and replace it with just the voice in your head. Then take that first step, by yourself, into a place that is not inherently safe. It might take a bit of gumption to stroll into the pub or your favorite Tex-Mex place sans date and feel fine about it, but in those cases the only thing at risk is feeling bad about other people looking at you with pity as you sip that whiskey or munch those nachos at a table for one. Even if you leave with a couple of smirks thrown your way, at least you're probably getting home intact.

A few years ago, I went on a solo trip in the Collegiate Peaks Wilderness of central Colorado, with plans to hike and scramble to the top of Missouri Mountain, a 14,000-foot high spot on a big ridge that encloses a beautiful alpine basin. I'd been there before, during a hike up Mount Belford years ago, so I was at least somewhat familiar with the area. But

Missouri Mountain would be new to me, and unlike that last trip here, I wasn't with nine other dudes.

It was also in an off-season time for hikers, and in the middle of the week. Added to that, the weather had been awful for several days – an unseasonal fall deluge flooded a number of Front Range towns near Denver, and higher up, those same storms had made for some particularly ugly conditions in the mountains. Farther south, where I was going, I was hoping to miss most of that nastiness.

I drove through the rain, seeing it clear off just before sunset. As darkness spread across the Rockies, I was wondering how alone I might be – would there be anyone at the trailhead? Or anyone on the mountain the next day?

The answer came as I pulled into the trailhead parking lot. Not a soul. Just an empty gravel lot and a whole lot of impenetrable darkness. I put the seats down in the back of the car, spread out some bedding, shut the hatch and hunkered down for the night.

Just because I was calling it a night doesn't mean my mind was shutting down. I ruminated over what the route might bring, and what the weather might do. I also contemplated the idea of maybe being the only person in Missouri Gulch Basin.

Let me state beforehand that plenty of people hike the Rockies alone and do so in complete safety. Many of my friends do. For me, it's more of a rarity. In any case, if you have the right preparation, experience and decision-making, you'll likely be fine doing the wilderness thing on your own.

Of course, that didn't quiet my mind.

You'll be taking off in the darkness, Bob. You know, the time when predators are most active.

You realize if you bust an ankle on the mountain, ain't no one gonna be coming for you for hours. Or maybe days. You know that, right?

Hey, and if you have to do an emergency bivvy on the mountain with a bum leg, you might just get caught in a blizzard. You ready for that, big boy?

Yep, those were the thoughts rolling through my head that night as I tried to lull myself to sleep with the mellowest songs on my playlist. The what-if scenarios were not implausible, mind you, but were seeded and fueled by mostly irrational fears. Mostly.

I didn't sleep much that night.

Sometime around 4:30, I got up, geared up and started up the steep switchbacks leading to Missouri Gulch Basin.

What I'd like to say is that all of my fears were unfounded, that the hike went flawlessly, that I watched the sun rise over the peaks and discovered a previously unseen-by-man meadow filled with unicorns farting rainbows and glitter. But alas, that was not the case.

Most of my fears were, indeed, unfounded. There were no freak accidents, no "127 Hours"-like predicaments, and no hostile wildlife mishaps aside from being buzzed by a rudely territorial hawk. Nonetheless, I suffered a bit on this one.

There have been days when I felt really strong on the mountain, where the altitude did not bother me and my legs were stout. This was not one of those days.

Added to that, the weather played this touch-and-go game with me almost the entire time. Below treeline, I hiked in thick fog that only broke sometime after dawn. While that cleared out, dark clouds swirled over the mountaintops, teasing at the possibilities of either unleashing a storm or maybe doing nothing at all. A light dusting of snow could be seen atop Mount Belford to my left, and straight ahead on the ridgeline of Missouri Mountain.

A lot of the signs seemed to point toward aborting this summit attempt. The voices in my head tended to agree.

This is just not your day. It's OK to turn around.

Those clouds look like they're getting darker. You don't want to be up there if a storm breaks out, do you?

No. You don't. Especially if some medical emergency happens. Because there's no one else here.

Yeah. You wanted this. Remember that. You wanted to be here on your own. So here you are, with the entire basin to yourself, without a soul within twenty miles of you and no cell service. If you keep going, you're just digging yourself a deeper hole. Idiot.

That's the strange thing about real solitude. You might be able to cut out the noise of the world, but then you have to deal with all the voices between your ears.

That, plus some of the implanted noise. Anyone who has done the least bit of hiking knows how easy it is to get a song stuck in your head, on continuous repeat of the catchiest, most annoying part. And then you get to have this happen to you for hours.

I got lucky this time – the song was "Molly's Chambers" from Kings of Leon. Good stuff. But it could have easily been something much more toxic. Madonna was once my nemesis. Today, it might be something from Taylor Swift's catchy little catalogue.

So here might be a worst-case scenario of implanted inner-mind noise while almost bailing on a mountain hike:

Man, I'm tired. A real bed sounds good right now.

"We-eee! Are never, ever, ever, getting back together!"

Holy shit this is steep. Is that angina I feel in my chest?

"We-eee! Are never, ever, ever, getting back together!"

Dear God. Look at those clouds. That has to be a storm. I'm gonna get caught in a thundersnow. And get jumped by a mountain lion. They'll find me in two years, picked over by those damn ravens, but at least this Clif bar will still be edible. A present for the search-and- rescue team who finds my sun-bleached bones.

"We-eee! Are never, ever, ever, ever.......getting back together!"

And so it goes, for hours. That's one heck of a combination of head noise that makes you want to quit. Sounds like fun, right?

But that's when the surroundings took over.

I coaxed myself up Missouri's northwest ridge, the last steep part of the hike before it levels off a tad on the upper ridgeline. Like I said earlier, Missouri Mountain encloses the basin from the south, forming a huge, stony amphitheater rising thousands of feet above the basin floor. Stunning visuals, to be sure.

What interrupted the self-defeating inner monologue wasn't at first what I saw, but what I heard. Somewhere way down below, a couple of pikas were chirping at one another, their high-pitched squeaks carrying throughout the basin and into my ears. A bit later, a raven's call, echoing hauntingly as its iterations bounced off towering walls of rock and throughout the airy, tundra-lined basin. Little things, to be sure. But enough to make me stop, listen, and appreciate the moment. Mentally speaking, it was juice to keep going.

Later on the summit ridge, those clouds were still there. The trail seemingly disappeared into a misty void, obscuring the summit. But it wasn't scary or anything like that. Instead, I might call it compelling. Marching into that gray mystery made tagging the summit that much more interesting. About thirty minutes later, I stood on top, checking out the views.

Dark clouds swirled above Mount Belford. Further away, the bulk of Mount Harvard, Colorado's third-highest peak, loomed. Closer in were the grassy slopes of two 13,000-foot mountains, Emerald Peak and Iowa Peak. Huron Peak took turns hiding, then emerging from the clouds, beautiful but demure.

I think you can learn a lot about yourself during times like this, where you test your body and will, and face down the noise that you can't run away from – the noise residing in your head. I won't lead you into believing this trip was an act of monumental fortitude or high-stakes adventure. Many, much tougher solo treks have been done, for certain. But I'll tell you this: Willing yourself up a 14,000-foot mountain when the weather, your body and your mind are telling you to quit and go home is much more significant than calling up the confidence to order dinner for one.

****

So how did this little trip end? After all, topping out is only halfway there.

As it turns out, I wasn't completely alone. A few other people dared the elements that day.

A couple of guys from Texas were about a half hour behind me on their own summit attempt. I spotted them navigating the one tricky part of the ridge, seeing if they could get through it without incident. They did, and about then is when I started my march down.

We stopped to talk for a few minutes – they'd been camping in the basin for a couple of days (I walked right by their campsite and didn't even see them), so, like me, they had been thoroughly unplugged from the outside world. We chatted a bit about college football (I delivered the bad news that their beloved Aggies had fallen to Alabama a couple of days earlier), then discussed the mountain before they decided they needed to get going toward the top.

I picked my way down the trail, hiking portions, "running" a few more, trying to make some time. I had a deadline of sorts to meet, a phone call to a friend to tell her that I was off the mountain and safe. If no call came, she was instructed to let the local authorities know.

Down in the basin, I ran into one other person. It was a lone woman, hiking with an orange, external-frame backpack with an empty milk jug dangling off the side, presumably for water. Real old-school stuff. We chatted for a couple of minutes, and she told me she was hiking the basin and over a pass in hopes of eventually walking to Buena Vista, a good twenty miles away. I thought I was kinda rad summiting Missouri Mountain on my own, but I had nothing on this gal. In my imagination, I figured she was probably a teacher or some other sort of professional who could get large chunks of time off to go on extended backpacking trips. And doing that on your own? She was on another level. She kept going up, I trudged on down.

I don't ever eat enough on these alpine treks. Altitude does not agree with my stomach. I find ways to get some grub down, but the calorie burn of an eleven-mile hike with 4,500 feet of gain wipes out those snacks quickly. So the fatigue sets in, and with miles to go, staying motivated turns into a challenge. It's not like you can stop and call for a ride. The "ride" is waiting for you at the trailhead. But you have to do something, anything, to keep your mind off how tired you are.

So I talked to myself a little. Not crazy talk, but it would be really out of place in "normal" life scenarios. So yes, that happens.

Sometimes I'd quietly sing a song, to get the internal jukebox off perpetual repeat. Maybe utter a prayer. I even resorted to counting switchbacks because, you know, counting stuff is a great way to pass time. Once I got low enough, I got to admire the colors of the turning aspens. And I found someone's misplaced dental retainer. Just one of many amazing and sometimes odd memories of what I saw that might have gone unnoticed in the company of others.

Hours later, I was back in my car headed toward civilization. I found a place with cell phone service and made the call to my friend to let her know I was

OK, filled up with gas and began the drive back to Denver. A burrito, a shower and a nap were on my mind, and in that order.

So while I was kicking rocks and catching my breath for the past couple of days, the world kept turning. As it turned out, I missed the news of the day – a mass shooting at a Navy station that ultimately kicked off another predictable social media/pundit newscast shoutfest over guns. Awesome.

At that point, I wished I was back in the bosom of wilderness, and away from the angst and outrage of "the real world." That noise reservoir? It was already filling up again, one drop at a time. It's a never-ending process, needing constant maintenance.

So on the cycle goes. The noise collects, it annoys, it fills up the bucket to the point where it needs to be emptied. When I've had my fill, the quiet indifference of the wild, absorbed on my own, sounds like paradise.

SIX: RISK

"Climb if you will, but remember that courage and strength are naught without prudence, and that a momentary negligence may destroy the happiness of a lifetime. Do nothing in haste; look well to each step; and from the beginning think what may be the end."

— *Edward Whymper, English mountaineer*

Among my friends, it's no secret which mountain range is my favorite. Hands down, it's the San Juans of southwestern Colorado. Being a bit of a mountain guy, they all appeal to me, but the San Juans stand out for all their wild beauty and remoteness. So many geologic forces shaped these wild peaks – uplift, volcanism and glacial carving – and the dramatic profiles within the range attest to some amazing natural creativity at work over the past several million years or so.

It's not like I've explored the whole range. I've been there often enough, but that particular alpine wilderness is extensive to the point of making my experiences there a mere sampling. That said, I'm not sure many people would blame me if I said my favorite mountain there – or anywhere, for that matter – is Wetterhorn Peak.

I love it for its accessibility, with a trailhead not far from Lake City, and a straightforward trail that leads to some fun scrambling to its 14,015-foot summit. It's no walk-up, but the climbing below the summit is such that most people can do it with a little courage and concentration on what they're doing on the rock. I'd climb this one again, and I'd gladly take any novice with me.

But more than that, Wetterhorn is beautiful, and dramatically so. Its sweeping southeast ridge rises gracefully skyward before abruptly shooting up, a vertical crop of rock marking its proud pinnacle. Wetterhorn's skyline is particularly fetching when viewed from the east, maybe from the top of little brother Matterhorn Peak, of which it which shares a rugged, spiny connecting ridge.

And then there's the view of the mountain from the north. From Wetterhorn Basin, the peak looks radically vertical, its north face shooting upward like a rocket. The San Juans contain gently sloping mountains, abrupt spires of rock, and everything in between, and Wetterhorn embodies a little of every aspect that makes the range so impossibly wonderful. I sound like a moonstruck teenager right now, all googly-eyed over the gorgeous cheerleader dancing away on the sideline. Sorry about that, but I can't help myself.

I'd been wanting to climb this one for several years, and had a shot at it a few years back, but for whatever reason, I went up another mountain instead. I guess I was a little spooked by some of the narrow, exposed ledges just under the summit, and I'd been in the middle of reading Aron Ralston's book *Between a Rock and a Hard Place*, the tale of when he'd been trapped in Blue John Canyon for 127 hours after his arm became pinned beneath a boulder. I wasn't worried about having to lop off my own arm on Wetterhorn, but I've got this thing about heights. Dreams of a blast of wind blowing me off that ledge and into an airy void danced in my head and sent me up Matterhorn Peak instead, a pretty but far-less demanding mountain. It was an irrational fear, but it's one of those quirks you deal with when heights aren't your jam.

A few years later, I got a chance to go with a group of people, including some friends from past hikes and climbs. David, an Air Force vet I'd met a year earlier on another San Juans climb, had been up Wetterhorn several times before, but most of the rest of the group had not. That would make it pretty special, but more so for Noel, who'd been turned away on this mountain years before when she got sketched out by sloppy snow on some of the steeper, trickier parts of the mountain. Since that day, she'd climbed many other, tougher mountains, but this one was, as she put it, her "nemesis."

We all had a few scores to settle on Wetterhorn. All of us had the experience and skill to do the job. But as is often the case, the mountain can throw things at you – challenges you don't expect – and humble you fast.

****

A lot of people wonder why folks tempt fate by exploring the mountains, but seriously, just look at them. Humans are drawn to high places. They are the settings of mythology and wonder. They tower over our lowland homes and promise a whole new view of the world. Such are the things that call us upward.

That allure is also what can get us into trouble. In an effort to escape our daily routines, many of us seek refuge in the peaks. But there is a reality of the high country that some of the more naïve (including me) occasionally miss.

Jon Krakauer probably summed it up best when he wrote (and I paraphrase) that mountains make bad receptacles for people's dreams. That's a nice way of saying the peaks don't care about you, your aspirations or your need for validation. Yes, the mountains seem to beckon. But don't think for a second that when you approach their lofty heights you're actually invited.

I'd explain it this way: You may have a day in the mountains where everything is going right. The weather is perfect, a true bluebird day. Your body is in prime condition and you're blasting up the route. New challenges are being tackled and mastered, and you even got the greatest summit selfie or group shot ever taken in the history of mankind. Even your GoPro footage looks like it could be made into the next great entry into the Banff or Reel Rock Tour film festivals.

And when you're done and everyone is at the pub snarfing a victory dinner with a beer or five, you may think that you and those titanic piles of rock have something special going on.

Don't fool yourself. Your next venture into alpine greatness might see that docile peak bear down on you like a lion, swallow you up and gnaw on your bones before ejecting you from its stony maw like an unwanted wad of spit, splayed out on its rocky apron and crying to God for help.

It's what mountains do. They do it randomly, with total dispassion, the same lack of concern they have when they let you enjoy your epic day of high country fulfillment. Mountains are beautiful, but they are harsh. Uncaring. Unmoved by our desires, dreams and thoughts. They'd just as soon see you die as let you pass by, taking in either scenario with the same, cold indifference.

Climb mountains enough and they will eventually reject your ambitions or, if you're unlucky, send you back to civilization on a stretcher.

I recently got turned back on one of the most frequently climbed mountains in all of Colorado, Longs Peak. It's a burly mountain that reigns over Rocky Mountain National Park, and even by its easiest route, it's a tough outing with a lengthy approach, boulder-hopping, and a good bit of steep, exposed and sustained scrambling to the summit. I went with a group that included four seasoned mountaineers, and a fellow flatlander named Craig from Kansas City.

We went into the day with a lot of optimism. Everyone was in good shape. A lot of experience in the mountains was within this team. But as we headed up, we began hearing from others coming down that overnight snows had done a number on the upper part of the route. The steepest, rockiest sections were now covered in rotten ice and slushy snow. We kept going, and at a critical go-or-no-go point called the Keyhole, we got a look at the route. It looked like it had been described. Worse yet, hellacious winds and gathering clouds whipped violently over the peak.

One look at that, and the most experienced guy in the group knew we were done. He said as much, and no one else needed any convincing, certainly not the two flatlanders. The mountain had its say, telling us "Not today," and we listened.

Needless to say, there are profound lessons to be learned in the mountains, even in the midst of failures like this. Truly transformational moments can happen. They can and do, something to which I can attest, even when the peaks treat you harshly.

And I think that's what makes the mountains so special to me. You go to work with expectations of getting paid. You go to church with the idea of learning something important. You go to concerts to get loud and to bars to blow off steam, and you go home to feel a sense of peace from the world that swirls around you.

But when I go to the mountains, I don't go with any expectations because I truly do not know what will happen when I'm there. I don't know if the weather will cooperate, if the peak will be too daunting, or even if I'll make it back at all. All of that is because the mountain will do what it's going to do regardless of my presence. A rock that stayed in place for a thousand years might move when you're there, but it also might not budge for a thousand more.

Whatever the mountain does, the manner in which you deal with it will be a measure of who you are in terms of skill, wit and toughness. Perhaps that's all we can know for certain, that the mountains will test us, but they'll do so with the nonchalance of something that has existed long before we were born, and will continue to stand tall long after we're gone.

****

Though we'd chosen to tackle Wetterhorn at the summer equinox, I'm not sure any of us were expecting quite as much snow as there was. Apparently, the San Juans had quite the winter and spring snowpack that year, which meant we'd be enduring a good deal of postholing up the lower slopes of the mountain. Fortunately, the sun wasn't out, meaning that the snow would be a little firmer underfoot, but with the temperatures in the low 40s everything was sure to get softer as the day wore on.

The hike up was uneventful, aside from a few jarring steps punching through softening, ice-encrusted snowfields. Everyone was in good spirits. We were making good time, the weather was holding out and the views were incredible. Anticipation of what was awaiting us at the summit pitch added to the excitement.

I was a different person going up Wetterhorn that day than I was a few years back when I spooked myself out of it. I'd done tougher mountains. But I wasn't here to necessarily test myself – I just really wanted to climb this mountain, one that had held my fascination for such a long time. It didn't hurt that I was in good company. Hikes and climbs like this are as much about the people you're with as they are the mountain itself. Some of our group was here to gain a confidence boost for future climbs, others to lead us along the way. For me, I was just happy to be there. There aren't any Wetterhorns in Oklahoma.

After a time, the easier hiking gave way to steeper slopes, and eventually we hit some light scrambles that traversed skinny, snow-filled gullies that ordinarily would present no troubles under dry conditions. The presence of slushy snow, however, made things more complicated. Those gullies, angled down toward the mountain's sizable west-facing cliffs, weren't the type of things on which you wanted to take a ride. We took our time going across those, kick-stepping as we went, and working our way toward more solid rock. There was one last, gently sloping snowfield under a rock formation called the Prow, and from there, it was a straightforward walk across a series of ledges leading to the summit pitch: a steep, solid stretch of rock where the climbing is a lot like ascending a ladder. Before long, we'd all topped out.

It was a cool moment. The views were ridiculously scenic, with snow gracing the summits of a sea of nearby peaks. I could make out several that I'd gone up before and many, many more I hadn't. You could come up here for years and not summit all of the San Juans.

Wetterhorn was a long time coming for me, and the slaying of a giant of sorts for Noel. The peak wasn't what spooked her on her last visit. It was the snow conditions, which were similar to what we saw that day. When all of us had made it to the top, we exchanged high-fives, munched on our food and drank in the sights. A couple of hungry marmots – plump, brown furballs resembling Mini-Me versions of a beaver – waited around for handouts or whatever crumbs we let fall. All said, Wetterhorn did not disappoint.

As with any mountain, it's not over until you get down. So we began the process of carefully downclimbing the rock, then traversing those airy but solid ledges before hitting the snowfield just under the prow. Upon crossing that, we came up on those pesky snow-filled gullies.

By now, the above-freezing temperatures had been around long enough that the snow softened even more. This is a concern going up, for sure. But going down, it becomes a lot more serious. Most mountain accidents happen on the downclimb, and even on a relatively safe peak like Wetterhorn, things can get dicey fast when bad traction and gravity converge.

Dave was the first to slip, but he caught himself quickly. It was enough to give him pause and let out a warning to the rest of us who were behind him.

As if on cue, I lost my footing as well. The kick-stepped piece of snow at my back foot crumbled beneath me, bringing me down to my butt with a thud. I slid about four or five feet, slowing my fall just enough to kick a foot out on the rock wall to my right, stopping the skid. It's a good thing, too. Had I kept going, I'm not sure where that trip would have ended. The little ribbon of snow I was on disappeared over an edge, and for all I knew, those massive cliffs on the west face of the mountain awaited. A fun trip to the top might have ended with someone calling search-and-rescue to come scrape my remains from the rocks hundreds of feet below.

The third guy to slip (it seems bad things happen in threes) was a fella named Durant who I'd met a couple of years earlier on a different mountain. Durant is a seasoned hiker and climber, a real nice guy who wouldn't be surprised by much.

But there's only so much you can do when your footing gives way and you start sliding down the hill.

We all saw it happen, and I can tell you that there are few things that will make you feel more helpless than watching someone accelerate down a snow slope. You just hope they can stop themselves before tragedy strikes.

Durant slid somewhere shy of a hundred feet before hitting a large rock. He got banged up pretty good, but otherwise was able to pop back up. I don't think he'd have gone off a cliff – not on that gully, anyway. The snow ended well before any cliff edge, meaning he would have been stopped by piles of sharp talus downslope. It would have been a rough landing, maybe more so than the one he experienced. A busted leg would have been a disaster on that part of the mountain, with no easy way to get an injured climber down. Any rescue operation would take several hours, and the possibility of bad weather moving in could have meant being stuck high on the mountain overnight. In any case, we all were relieved he was OK, and were glad to be past those gullies. Mishaps like these are why you wear helmets, put spikes on your boots and carry ice axes. It's a pain lugging that stuff around, but you will definitely miss it if and when you need it and it's not there.

Those few minutes traversing the snow gullies changed the mood considerably. All of us remarked how fortunate we were that nothing worse happened, and in an odd twist, what happened there actually confirmed the initial fears that plagued Noel the last time she was here.

Such is the nature of mountains. In one moment, they'll bless you with an amazing visual payoff and an emotional lift that comes from victory, then abruptly snatch it away. The best-case scenario is that you are humbled, beat up, and maybe a little frazzled but still alive.

The worst: Everyone reads about you the next day.

****

Not long ago, I was reading a book titled *One Mountain, Thousand Summits*, a tome about the 2008 K2 climbing disaster. The writer, Freddie Wilkinson, makes a point of not only documenting what occurred on the mountain, but also what happened around the world in response to the tragedy. In doing so, he followed media reporting – and reader comments – on the internet.

For the sake of context: Eleven people died directly and indirectly from a serac collapse high on K2, one of the worst disasters in mountaineering history.

Some of the online comments quoted in the book are as follows:

"Spirit of exploration? Please. K2 has been climbed before. Many times. It was 'discovered' a long time

ago. Climbers today climb 8,000-meter peaks for one reason: themselves."

Another was even more blunt:

"This was not a voyage of discovery; it was an ego trip, as most mountain ascents are today."

Similar sentiments were made after the 1996 Everest disaster, and just about any other report of a mountaineering accident that includes someone's death.

Let's go beyond the callousness that goes into writing screeds like these. There is a deeper philosophical question to be posed here: Do these armchair quarterbacks have a point?

Why do we climb mountains? For that matter, why do we do a lot of the physically challenging and at-times risky things we do?

The great mountains of the world have been climbed. The poles have been reached. The jungles and deserts have, for the most part, been traversed and explored.

And yet we still climb these peaks, journey to the poles and travel in some of the most inhospitable environments in the world. Often, people do this with a twist: trying to be the "first" at something (oldest, youngest, first woman, first blind person, etc.), and admittedly, some of these efforts are done for publicity's sake. But more commonly, we merely retrace paths already taken – often many times before – only for our own benefit.

I can relate. Every mountain I've climbed and every route I've taken has already been done, maybe hundreds or thousands of times.

So outside of space and the oceans, much of the age of exploration has come to an end, the purposes of which have gone beyond the greater good and now veer toward the strictly personal.

So why bother? Why risk injury and death to climb?

I set the book down and let this question rattle around in my brain for awhile, and then let the thought broaden. Mountaineering accidents, particularly high-profile mishaps, get a lot of attention. News articles, TV specials and books usually follow. But there are other things we do that draw parallels.

People die running marathons. Not often, but it happens. Why run a marathon on Pikes Peak? People have had heart attacks and dropped dead trying that race. Even in my city's local marathon there has been a fatality. The people who have died in these races possessed, for the most part, the fitness level needed for the task, but died anyway.

I know that's extreme, but there are other less severe yet still noteworthy examples of how people have suffered incredibly by trying to run 26.2 miles or more. Training for such races can do a whole lot of damage to your body, consume much of your time and energy and change your lifestyle in ways that are not always positive.

Here's a fact: The overwhelming number of people who run ultramarathons, marathons, half marathons, 15ks, 10ks and 5ks do so without even the slightest chance of winning. Or placing high. Or winning their gender, age group or whatever. It is supposed to be a race, right? Why run a race you have no shot of winning? Or no shot of even being the slightest bit competitive?

Let's move into other sports, say football. It's a great game, one of my favorites. Pro football in particular interests me because it is the game played at the highest level by the biggest, fastest and most skilled athletes in the sport. It's such a difficult challenge to even win one game, not to mention a championship.

But at what cost? The concussion debate has been raging for a few years now. But there is a host of other injuries these guys suffer on top of that, maladies that leave these fantastic physical specimens barely able to walk, much less run, when they hit middle age. Obviously, the money is a major reason why these men do this, but when the crowds no longer cheer and all you're left with is a broken body (and in some cases, mind), can you say that those years of abuse were worth it?

Here's another question:

What's the alternative?

The alternative is not to pursue the difficulties of planning, training for and finally attempting a mountain climb. The alternative is to stay inside, substitute your running shoes for a pair of house slippers and spend yet another mindless day on the couch watching TV or playing video games (which often portray characters doing epic things. Kind of ironic). The alternative is to never plumb the depths of your abilities to see how far you can take your God-given talents.

If you never push yourself to see how strong you can be, you'll never be strong. And that's not just in terms of physical strength, but mental and emotional strength as well. These tests tell us how tough we can be and often lead us to personal growth that can't be replicated in the world of the easy and mundane.

None of us will ever be the first to climb Everest, K2 or thousands of other peaks. We won't be the first to reach the north or south poles. Almost no one in this world of seven billion people will set a new world-record marathon time, and only the tiniest fraction of all athletes will do something as comparatively normal as winning a long-distance race. Sorry to burst your bubble.

But so what? These are the ways we measure ourselves, promote growth and even inspire others to try and do great things. Obviously, some pursuits are riskier than others, but you won't see me discouraging people from such endeavors, provided they weigh the risks, prepare thoroughly, and do so with a healthy degree of humility for the task at hand.

Lace 'em up, people. Buckle that chin strap. Climb on. If you want to criticize that, then enjoy your time on the couch. I'm sure it will be a faithful companion on your journey to the perfectly average for some time to come. For those who choose to go out and "do" things, you never know what reward awaits you when the challenge is accepted, then met.

****

Getting clear of those gullies proved to be a relief. You spend a lot of physical energy going up and down a mountain, but you can't discount the mental energy that's expended when dealing with stressful situations. Seeing Durant's slide, and feeling your own kicksteps break up underneath your own feet, definitely qualifies. Getting through that, all we had left to do was march our way down gentler slopes on tired legs, a situation made more acute every time we punched knee-deep through a thin crust of ice and into the soft snow underneath. I've mentioned the term "postholing" before, and what it means in practical terms is burning a whole lot more energy with every step you take, fighting through snow, falling down, scratching yourself up and otherwise making a tired walk downhill that much more miserable.

But then, help arrived.

Oftentimes when I'm on a mountain, I joke about wishing a zip line would magically appear, making that hours-long trudge back to the trailhead disappear in a matter of minutes. No such device exists on Colorado's high summits, but during the right time of year you get the next best thing: The slick surface of snow that was so treacherous higher up the peak is a whole lot more inviting on longer, mellower slopes devoid of cliffs.

A small number of people ski the 14ers, meaning they climb the peak, skis strapped to their backs, and then click in, point their tips downslope and ride all the way to the bottom. Absent skis or a snowboard, the next best thing is a glissade.

"Glissade" is a fancy sounding word for sitting down and sliding downhill on your butt. It's usually done using an ice axe to help you steer or stop, and if an axe isn't available, you can use whatever tool you have available – maybe a trekking pole, or perhaps a climbing helmet. In any case, once you get going it can be a wild ride to the bottom. Think of all those times you went sledding as a kid, and a glissade is just like that, except you're on your butt, and the ride might cover the length of several football fields. You pick up speed, you hit bumps, you get a little out of control and the wind blows over your face and into your ears. I don't speak or read French, but I think the translation for "glissade" in colloquial English is "wheeee!"

So that's what we did. Well, some of us anyway. The hardier souls in our group were in shorts, so a glissade down the slope would likely result in the biggest, coldest atomic wedgie known to humanity. Durant also took a pass for a couple of reasons. One, he was bruised and battered from his incident higher on the mountain, and two, it's probably safe to say he'd gotten all the sliding on snow he wanted for the day.

A fella named Dan went first. He ran toward the slope and plunged himself downward, and in an instant, he was gone, shooting down the mountain like a torpedo. We soon followed suit. I have to say, there are far less pleasant ways to lose a thousand feet of elevation, and most of them are much slower. Though my tailbone was sore for a few weeks (I did mention that it got bumpy), it was totally worth it. So much speed, so much fun, and we shaved off at least a half hour of hiking time. A decent trade-off, I'd say.

It was also a sweet contrast to what had happened earlier, using the same qualities that snow and gravity threw our way to our peril earlier in the day for a bit of fun now. Hollering all the way down, whooping it up and high-fiving each other at the bottom was a great way to break the negative tension that took over during and immediately after the gullies.

I like to look at it as if the mountain had snarled at us during those tense moments just under the summit, baring its teeth, letting us know that it was no mere hill or amusement park attraction. It was a wild place, free to do whatever it wanted with us, mere insects in its immeasurably old and big life. But then she showed us a kinder side later on, allowing us to leave with neither dread nor hubris, but something closer to humble appreciation. We were glad we were there, pleased no one got seriously hurt, and grateful for having climbed it.

I don't know how dangerous Wetterhorn is, at least in comparison to other mountains. It's not the Tetons or Everest or Rainier, but it's not a gentle hill in your local park and certainly comes without handrails. Many people have climbed it; I personally don't know of anyone who has died trying. But certainly someone *could* die on Wetterhorn, just as people have perished on far less demanding peaks in the Rockies and elsewhere. You could also die tomorrow on your morning commute, or putting up Christmas lights, or any number of ways far more ordinary.

We're not promised tomorrow. Only now. And that's why people climb mountains. There is a huge difference between living in the "now" while you're scaling a rock wall with a bunch of air beneath you and living in the "now" while playing *Call of Duty*, binge-watching *Stranger Things* or overdosing on Pinterest. You choose your now, and you should do so with careful thought because it is a commodity of which we are given a very finite supply.

SEVEN: MIKE

"Love God, love people."

– Mike Doucette, March 21, 2011

If you spent any time with my brother Mike, you'd learn quickly what it meant to go deep. Mike's not one for small talk.

I was seated in a chair as he was stretched out in bed. The TV was on, showing a basketball game between the Denver Nuggets and some other team I can't recall. Denver was getting the best of them. Otherwise, things were pretty quiet. Our discussion turned to the mountains.

Mike liked to ask questions. I think he could have been a reporter, but his mind was gifted in so many other things, his talent so broad. Ultimately it was the computer field that attracted his intellect instead of the interesting but not-so profitable world of news media. And still, the questions came. He continually probed people's minds.

We were talking about the peaks, and particularly, which mountain was our favorite. I don't remember what I said then. My list of peaks isn't that long, but it's changed since this conversation took place. I'm sure I stated my reasons why I liked it – the views, the ascent, the people I was with – and then turned the question back on him.

Mike's peak list was broader than mine. Still is. Among those ascents are some pretty tough routes, including one that Outside Magazine dubbed as one of America's most dangerous hikes, Longs Peak. I'd hardly call that route a "hike" – even by its easiest route, there's a fair amount of scrambling and climbing to reach its summit. Mike told me that when he climbed Longs, especially when he hit the final pitch known as The Homestretch, "I felt like I was really climbing a mountain."

And yet that was not his favorite.

Instead, Mike chose Quandary Peak.

Those of you who know Colorado's peaks understand there is a substantial difference between the two. Both top out at more than 14,200 feet, but that's where the similarities end. For those of you who don't know, here's how I'd describe Quandary:

It's distinctive in its appearance. Driving in from Breckenridge or Dillon, its long, broad, sweeping east ridge is unmistakable, like that of an enormous whale breaching the waves. Most people choose that ridge to gain its summit. There are tougher, riskier routes on the mountain's west ridge and along its flanks, but the east ridge is the most popular, mostly because it's the most accessible and least difficult way to get to the top. Quandary's east ridge is scenic, not too steep, and, relatively speaking, one of the safer routes you can take up any of Colorado's high peaks.

That's why Mike liked it. Quandary Peak was the one go-to mountain where he could take a novice hiker and see that person enjoy a first-timer mountain experience. It is in that answer you get to the heart of my brother.

As much as Mike enjoyed exploring new places in the high country, he preferred taking folks to areas where he'd already been. To him, it was about seeing the look on their faces when they reach that signature view on the mountain, the final march to the summit and the high-fives back at the trailhead. He looked forward to sharing his knowledge of the mountain, about how to pace yourself, what gear to bring, what food to eat, and the little details of alpine environments that a lot of folks would miss if they were left to their own devices. Mike lived for that kind of thing. So as aesthetically pleasing as Longs Peak might be, Quandary Peak fit Mike's style because it was a place where he could more easily share his love of the mountains with others.

Mike's answer fit his nature perfectly. Most of the time, Mike was thinking about others – the barista at his local Starbucks, the troubled teen sitting alone at church, or the homeless guy he saw on his way to work – all of these people got his attention and his kindness. This example gave me something to think about when it came to planning what mountain I'd like to do next.

We chatted awhile longer as the night breezed by. What mountain would we like to do together next? Where would it be? We both mentioned Mount Whitney in California, but ultimately Mike settled on going back to his old favorites, and taking with him anyone who was willing to give this whole 14er thing a try.

The thought of it was uplifting, but also far away from where we were. The bed he was in had a higher price tag than my car. His room, an entire city and several miles away from home. I had to wash my hands and put on a fresh hospital smock just to be in there.

Mike was sick. His once muscled and rugged body was ravaged by illness and the subsequent treatment, his eyes dulled to the point where the images of the basketball game on TV were just bright, moving blobs. Whereas he once could pull off twenty-mile alpine hikes, it was now an arduous task just to make it to the bathroom. Quandary Peak may as well have been K2.

Still, it was a hopeful discussion on what had been, overall, a pretty good day. I got a sense that he really looked forward to leaving that hospital, getting himself back in shape and making a charge up another Rocky Mountain peak, with an anxious little crew of followers in tow.

Or perhaps he was just telling me things he knew I needed to hear. Like I said, Mike was always thinking of others.

****

Michael William Doucette was born on December 8, 1963, the second child to a New Englander father and a German immigrant mother. For his entire life, from childhood to manhood, Mike was an overcomer, finding achievement where a lot of folks glumly give up. Going through his life, the pattern is unmistakable.

He wasn't a terribly big guy. Like all of the Doucette brothers, he was a little small as a kid. As a youth, he dealt with asthma. Plenty of forces worked against him, telling him, "you can't do this."

And then he just did it anyway.

Mike's intensity stood out. He tapped into that trait to earn a spot on his high school football team, despite being undersized for his position. He was a hard runner, and for any running back, courage is a must. You have to be brave to run into a wall of much bigger dudes whose sole goal is to stop you in your tracks and make you think twice about getting back up.

You didn't want to fight Mike. He could keep his cool for only so long, but when he broke, he broke big. A flash of anger would beam from his icy green eyes, and he'd unleash a tempest of punches that felled bigger kids all the way through his teen years. The only guy I ever saw who could corral that ferocity was my dad, and he's a third-degree black belt.

I remember shadowboxing with him when I was a scrawny little teen, and he was a muscled-up college guy. I accidentally didn't pull one jab soon enough and bopped him on the nose. He was cool for a second, but then that icy flash lit his gaze, and the next thing I knew I was being hurled across the room like a ragdoll. I'm really glad it ended there.

Being a goal-oriented dude, Mike constantly tested himself. He would see how long he could jump rope while holding his breath. How many push-ups he could do in an hour. How long he could submerge himself in the pool before coming up for air. Weightlifting suited him well, as there are few more objective tests of physicality than seeing how much weight you can pick up off the ground, push off your chest or load on your back.

This goal-oriented fixation led to plans. Mike was fit, and his vision razor sharp, better than 20/20. Soon after enrolling at Colorado State University, he joined the school's Air Force ROTC program. He wasn't going to settle for being part of the group. He was going to be an officer. And not just any officer: He set his sights on being a pilot. Throughout school, he tested near or at the top of his ROTC class, and that dream of piloting an F-16 drew closer every day.

As was typical of his life, an obstacle arose. A routine physical revealed a benign heart murmur – no big deal for his long-term future, but in the cockpit of a fighter jet pulling multiple Gs it could be fatal. In short, his pilot dreams were done before he ever got the chance to hit the tarmac. So faded his planned career in the Air Force.

But that massive reservoir of intensity would not be held back. Mike had to start over, to find something he could move toward. He was newly married and possessed a degree that wasn't going to take him anywhere, so he went back to school, studying computer programming. He worked part- and full-time jobs at crappy hours for low pay, earning enough money to pay rent in a basement apartment and stay in school. Mike hit a home run on his grades, built a reputation and landed a programming gig for Conoco in Houston, leaving behind the dead-end jobs of his college days and embarking on what would become a successful career in the tech industry.

Computers were a good fit for Mike. I cannot begin to describe how smart this guy was. Figuring out how to make a program work was the exact type of intellectual puzzle he needed to keep his attention.

Like I said earlier, he was not a small-talk guy. He enjoyed deep conversations about life and spirituality. I can remember talking to him about God, and how he was absolutely positive that he could find a way to prove the veracity of his Christian faith. He chased that rabbit as far as he could, and after becoming disheartened by his inability to do so, fell into a bit of a funk. Yet another crisis – this one on an existential level – confronted him.

I think this is where he grew the most. Upon giving up that quest, he realized that faith was not about finding an empirical solution to a problem, but rather finding a trust in something not seen. As he settled into that reality, Mike took a huge step forward as a man. He'd always been generous, kind and helpful, but now there was something more substantive, even muscular, behind it. He had his wife, his two kids, his home and his career. And now, a real sense of purpose. From here on out, his commitment to people and to God came first.

I guess the "people first" portion of that commitment explains his Quandary Peak fixation.

****

If you could describe Mike's intellect in one word, "powerful" would be a great choice. I'd prefer to use a few more terms. If you were to equate Mike's mind to a muscle, it would be Schwarzenegger-like in proportions.

As it turns out, his physique wasn't far off from that description, either. Like everything about Mike, it wasn't something that came easy, and was born from life crises.

As a youth, Mike was an athlete. He kept that part of his life alive well into adulthood, lifting weights, riding his bike, playing sports and generally trying to keep himself fit. His career eventually took him back to Colorado, working at a large tech firm and earning reasonably decent coin for his labors.

But as was common for a lot of guys in their mid- to late-thirties, the hard body from high school got a little soft around the middle. The weight gain, plus work stress and age, also did a number on his blood pressure and cholesterol. A steady diet of drugs to combat those problems left him feeling listless and old. So a new challenge arose, and Mike was glad to accept. He decided to find a way to overcome those health issues and kick the pharmaceuticals to the curb. Which, of course, he did.

Mike went from 210 pounds with a total cholesterol level in the upper 200s to a ripped 165 pounds with a cholesterol level number to match. He accomplished this in twelve weeks.

I remember trying to work out with Mike a few times when I visited him in Denver. It was one of those experiences where we loaded on a whole ton of weight for him, then peeled it off for me. We must have gotten almost as much exercise changing iron plates as we did from performing the exercises in that day's chosen workout. It's not like I'm a slouch in the weight room – he'd just taken it to another level. Mike's intensity was channeled into a fine-tuned discipline of training and diet, one where he proudly boasted that he would not go "one tic-tac" off his nutrition program.

He was stoked about his success and wanted to take it further by trying out competitive bodybuilding. He wanted to go the all-natural route, which would not only keep him healthier, but provide a bigger challenge.

And then, another setback. While playing in an indoor soccer league, he collided with another player, breaking his ankle and tearing some knee ligaments in his left leg, ending his season and, for the time being, other athletic goals he had in mind.

Or so we thought.

The injury happened in March of 2003. Like he had done many times before, Mike tapped into that deep pool of intensity, honed it to a fine point and embarked on an aggressive rehab program aimed at not only getting him back on his feet, but also back on track with his goals.

By July, he was standing atop Wheeler Peak, a 13,000-foot mountain in New Mexico, waiting on me and my friend Rick to join him. He'd hung back with us until the summit was within sight, then ran the rest of the way – a good quarter mile – to the top. The two guys with healthy knees huffed and puffed their way to meet him about ten minutes later.

Mike competed in several bodybuilding shows in the years to come, getting a little bigger, a little stronger, and little more defined each time he stepped on stage. He also coached people who were new to the sport –

typical Mike, teaching, giving, and helping people succeed.

In the midst of competing, he kept doing awesome things – earning patents for his professional work, winning trophies onstage, climbing mountains in Colorado. A few years back, me, Mike, and our brother Steve met up to hike a couple of the 14ers – Mount Biesrstadt and Quandary Peak, which would be the first two Steve had ever done. The three of us hung out all week, hiked the peaks, ate pizza until we could consume no more, and talked about life. It was a cool gathering of brothers, all grown and well into our adult lives, but Mike was definitely our ringleader, leading conversations in the same smooth, easy way he guided us up those mountains.

About a year later, he was with a couple of friends who were intent on hiking Mount Belford, then crossing a ridge to tag nearby Mount Oxford. It was a big day, with a steep, tough approach hike, then many hours above treeline. Strangely, Mike wasn't feeling it that day, so he decided to settle for Belford and call it good.

Tiredness began to become more prevalent in his everyday life. Exercises that were once routine became difficult. Uncharacteristically, Mike was getting more prone to catching colds. He went on a vacation to Hawaii with his family, stayed in an amazing place and even dealt with a near-crisis while at sea on a small boat. It was exciting to read his account of that trip, but he came back wondering why he'd been feeling so off.

Around that time, his brother-in-law was having heart troubles. Mike got to thinking about his heart murmur and wondered if there was a chance he was suffering from a similar condition. So he went to the doctor and got tested.

In the summer of 2010, maybe a month after that Hawaii trip, Mike left me a message, saying we needed to talk. When I called him, he told me how he'd been feeling, what prompted him to get tested and what he'd learned.

The heart disease he'd feared was an illusion. But his next battle was quite real. He'd been diagnosed with myelodysplastic syndrome, a type of cancer. It was likely that he'd had it for some time, and that he needed to start treatment immediately.

****

I can trace my love of the outdoors right back to my family. It's not like that should be any huge surprise: Who isn't a product of their upbringing? All my family has shaped who I am: My music tastes, what I eat, staying in shape, and a sometimes overpowering sense of loyalty. These are traits that were planted like seeds, growing into who I eventually became.

Mike played a big role in expanding my outdoorsiness. When we were younger, we'd go fishing in the streams and ponds in northern Illinois, looking for pike, bass or whatever we could catch. Later, we'd do the same in a quest for trout in the beaver ponds and mountain creeks of Colorado's high country.

But as time passed and adulthood hit, career took priority. Mountain dreams faded a bit as I rushed to meet deadlines and sought out that next gig that would finally tell me I'd made it. Somewhere around then, I had conversations with Mike about his adventures in the mountains.

He described bushwhacking through tangled willows, tricky stream crossings and sweeping views, about white-knuckled ridge traverses between peaks that were exhilarating and nerve-wracking, feats that he was glad he did, but would question doing again. As we poked through photographs of these places and let those tales unfold, a fire relit underneath me.

Why can't this be me? Why not now?

In 2002, when my wife Becca and I were vacationing in Red River, New Mexico, I got up one morning and looked at the ski mountain that overlooks the town. It rose to an elevation of about 10,000 feet.

Why not me? Why not now? So I left the lodge and trudged to the top of the hill, picking up a little more than 1,000 feet of elevation and getting a nice summit view as a payoff. It was summer, but the resort operators were taking people on rides up the ski lift to the top. Some of the people in the chair lifts saw me hiking up, commenting on how glad they were to have chosen the ride over the walk. It made me feel a little badass.

Back at the lodge, I paged through a guide of local hikes, and it mentioned the trails leading up to the top of nearby Wheeler Peak, the state's highest point at 13,153 feet. The guide rated the trek as "very strenuous," and twenty miles round trip. A couple of days later, I went to that trail and started walking, just to check it out. It was a short outing, but I vowed I'd be back.

A year later, I got in shape and returned to Wheeler Peak with Mike and my friend, Rick, who was also looking to try this mountain thing. We did the East Fork Trail in a shade over nine hours, with Mike leading the way.

If the stories and pictures from Mike's past hikes and climbs rekindled something in me, Wheeler Peak turned it into a bonfire. I've always loved the outdoors, but finding those mountain summits would become an obsession.

The next year, he was there with me and a big group of friends to hike our first 14er, Mount Belford. Two weeks later, Mike and I topped out on Mount Shavano. And a year after that, we were atop Mount Elbert, Colorado's highest point and the second-highest peak in the lower forty-eight states.

The mountains would always be a good touchpoint for Mike and I. As I did more, we could compare experiences on a deeper level. It's safe to say if not for Mike's stories, I'm not sure I'd have stepped one foot onto an alpine trail, maybe never gotten into trail running, and probably would have missed out on one of the biggest blessings to have come across my path.

That's what inspirational people do. They lead by their actions, find a way to express that to others, and prompt change. It's part of what made Mike great.

****

There is a feeling you get when you learn a loved one has cancer. I'd call it helplessly urgent. The urgency lies in the fact that you recognize a problem, want to fix that problem, and want to do it now. Cancer is one of those things that demands attention.

But you're helpless, for the most part, because there isn't much most of us can do. It's not like a car that broke down that you can fix, or a $500 loan you can get in a pinch. Cancer is something the experts must handle, and it takes a while to figure out how to do that. We all waited for Mike to hear from the doctors what he was in for and what they hoped to do about it. After that, there might be something we could do to help, but until then, it was many days of helplessly urgent prayers and worry.

Myelodysplastic syndrome, or MDS, is a lot like leukemia, so much so that for years it had been given the misnomer of pre-leukemia. It affects the body's bone marrow, compromising a person's ability to produce blood cells. If you get sick with MDS, the initial signs are easy to miss. You feel a little more tired. You might notice that you catch colds more frequently than normal. As the condition worsens, the fatigue gets more serious. Climbing stairs might be hard, or you get winded by tasks that didn't used to bother you much. And it seems like you're rolling over from one little bug to the next, never quite feeling right.

Dying from MDS is basically a slow wind-down. The fatigue comes from a decreasing number of red blood cells, causing a lack of oxygen going to your muscles and organs. The increased frequency of illnesses comes from a lack of white blood cells, the body's sentries that fight invasive bacteria, viruses, or anything else that doesn't belong. And then there are the platelets. If you lose those, the ability to clot is compromised. Suffering from MDS is a lot like being an anemic hemophiliac with some of the symptoms of AIDS. Eventually, internal organs will suffer from oxygen and nutrient deficiencies, and any little bruise or cut can be deadly serious. Diseases we sleep off with over-the-counter drugs can become life-threatening.

You can mitigate these problems to a point, but all the precautions in the world eventually fail – in a contest against an untreated case of MDS, the cancer always wins.

Like leukemia, the solution is a bone marrow transplant. That in itself is touchy business.

There are a couple of ways to do it. First off, you have to find a genetic match. Once one is found, you can do a direct transplant into the patient, or, in the alternative, opt for a stem cell transplant. The first option can be painful for both the donor and the recipient. The second – much less so. Stem cell transplants are relatively new, and when you hear it described, it sounds part genius, part magic.

The stem cell transplant, in basic terms, works a lot like a blood transfusion. It's far less invasive than a bone marrow transplant, giving it special allure. I'm not a scientist, but how it was explained to me was that once the donated stems cells are transplanted and grafted into the body, they immediately know to go to work to produce new, healthy bone marrow, which in turn leads to production of all those vital blood cells.

The tricky part is that you must be healthy (no fever or lingering infections) for the process to begin. Once you're given the go-ahead, chemotherapy is used to kill off your existing bone marrow tissue until it's wiped out. When that happens, your body has no defenses to fight infections. Anyone who visits the patient – be they a doctor, nurse or relative – must wash their hands, put on a surgical mask and don a hospital gown before even entering the patient's room. Leave the room, and you have to peel all that stuff off, toss it, and then start the process anew before re-entering. Kids in school are often discouraged from visiting at all because of the germs they catch from being around scores or hundreds of other children and whatever illnesses they might be carrying.

If all goes well and the donated stem cells do their job, you'll see a surge of newly created blood cells within days. If that happens, you have a successful grafting of the transplanted stem cells.

Unfortunately, that's just the beginning. With any transplant, you have to watch to see if the body accepts – or rejects – the new tissue in its midst. Organ rejection occurs when the antibodies in the blood stream see the new, transplanted organ as a foreign substance. If that happens, the organ often gets attacked by the body's natural defenses. This is a common issue with organ transplant patients, something routinely treated with medication. But generally speaking, the closer the genetic match, the better chance the patient can go back to a normal, healthy life.

With MDS and the stem cell transplant, the script is flipped. By killing off the old bone marrow and growing new tissue from a donor stem cell, you're hoping that the new antibodies don't react badly. If they do, it won't be just one organ they see as a foreign enemy. It will be all of them. And if that happens, the transplanted tissue will wage an all-out war on everything it sees. There are ways to treat this, too, but you hope the intensity of this condition – called graft versus host disease – isn't too severe.

Mike's doctors suggested the stem cell transplant. My sister Shiela, my brother Steve and myself were tested to see if we'd be a suitable match. None of us were. So the search field was widened, and lo and behold, we were told a match was found.

In late November 2010, the procedure started. We waited anxiously to see if the transplant graft was successful, and sure enough, all of the blood cell numbers started rising, very slowly at first, then rocketing through the roof. We were excited to hear this news, that Mike, ever the battler, was going to beat this thing.

We weren't ready for what came next.

The early symptoms of graft versus host disease, or GVH, first showed up as the inability to keep any food down, then diarrhea. Then blisters began to appear on his skin. Mike's eyes became cloudy, taking his eagle-sharp vision down to near blindness. The pain on his skin and in his gut was severe, and sleep rarely came. Doctors measure GVH's severity on a scale of one to four, with four being the worst.

Mike was a four.

I took in this news from afar, hundreds of miles away, hearing about how bad Mike felt but not seeing it, therefore unable to understand how desperate things were. My sister and parents were there, and had been for a couple of months, to help Mike's family at home and be there for him at the hospital as his treatment progressed.

They knew. And when Mike told them he was ready to stop treatment, my sister called me.

On a cold January night, Shiela explained to me what was happening to Mike, that he didn't want to continue with his treatment, and how that meant that he was basically saying he wanted to die. That's the problem with the regimen he was on – once it starts, there was no turning back, and if you stopped the treatment the new antibodies coursing through your veins would finish you off.

"It's serious," she told me. "You better come now."

I remember exactly where I was when I got that call. I was sitting in my car outside a Walgreens, waiting for my wife to pick up a prescription. We'd just picked up some sandwiches from a local deli. I hit the "end call" button, put the phone down and punched the inside of the door three times, yelling, "DAMMIT!" to no one in particular. I knew it was bad, but the thought hadn't crossed my mind that Mike wasn't going to survive. Yet here it was. I'd get to Denver as fast as I could, try to convince Mike to fight on a little longer, or use the coming days to say goodbye.

It was hard to swallow. I'd seen Mike about four months earlier, before the treatments had started. He was in a different hospital, doing tests. He looked a little pale, but still powerfully built, sharp in his mind, and determined. He might have been ill, but could still bench press a truck. He worked from his hospital bed, wrote on a blog and talked about book ideas for when he got through this ordeal.

Months later, when I saw him again, that muscled frame had withered. His skin was gray, and his belly distended. Those sharp, icy eyes were dulled, almost in the way you'd see with someone who had a bad case of cataracts. When he spoke, his words came out slowly, barely audible.

The cancer had made Mike seriously ill. But it was the "cure" that was killing him.

I was relieved to hear that in between the days when my sister called and when I got there, Mike had a change of heart. He'd heard some encouraging reports, and with his family rallying around him, he wanted to fight on. I'd taken a week off from work to be there, all too glad to be around to visit with him, encourage him and do whatever I could.

Part of his therapy was doing daily exercises. Now here was somewhere I could help. As weakened as he was, he could still do resistance training with thick rubber bands, even from his bed. He could also do exercises where I'd push against his hands and he'd resist, or he would push against mine and I'd resist. He still had strength in him.

Sometime that week, I got a call from my employer, telling me they'd had a layoff. I took the call in

Mike's hospital room, darted out into the hall and absorbed the bad news. I was one of about forty-something people getting canned. Pretty rotten news, and definitely part of a swell downward trend in my own life at that time, but on the bright side, it would give me more time to spend with Mike.

I returned home at the end of the week, cleared out my desk and said my goodbyes. Within a couple of weeks, I was back in Denver. I didn't tell Mike about the job loss, figuring he had enough on his plate. So I spent my days looking for work and afternoons and nights at the hospital.

Aside from the exercises, Mike would like for people to read him stories from the newspaper. His eyesight was improving, but not to the point where he could read newsprint. I'd read him the big news or sports stories of the day, paging through The Denver Post and USA Today, and we'd discuss what was going on. Mike's body was weak, but that mind was still sharp.

Other improvements came. For weeks, he'd been tube fed, but now he was at the point where he could put down solid foods. Soon his exercise regimen included sitting up, then standing by his bedside. Then, short walks to the bathroom or down the hall. I'm a hopeless optimist, and seeing this fanned those happy flames. Mike wasn't out of the woods, but something was happening. Something good. And based on some of the stories we'd heard about other MDS survivors, I started thinking about how, maybe in a year or two, we'd do that Mount Whitney climb. And we'd bring Steve, because another bro-trip was clearly the right thing to do.

One night, Mike and I were talking about great places to live. I mentioned a few places I liked, but he gently shook them off. He liked the idea of Costa Rica, where the climate was good, you could grow your own food, and you'd be far from the weird complications of modern American life. Visions of Costa Rican bungalows and jungle hikes up Central American mountains danced in my head. "Yeah, we could do this," I told him. "I should probably pick up a little Spanish."

That was a good day. Mike had his bad days, where he was loopy from the drugs or just plain tired, but this wasn't one of them. We talked for hours, watched the Nuggets on TV and talked about their players. Eventually the game ended and he was feeling sleepy, so we called it a night. I drove home, feeling good about what I saw as the inevitable conclusion – Mike would be leaving that hospital on his own two feet, ready to tackle the rest of his life.

I like to remember that day, or specifically, that night. Of all the days I'd had with Mike since his illness, that was the one where I felt the most hopeful. But it was fleeting. His GVH had been managed, even beaten back a bit. But as it turned out, that peaceful evening was a temporary reprieve. The tempest was far from finished.

GVH is persistent. If the case is severe, it doesn't stop attacking the digestive tract, and eventually, that never-ending assault finds weaknesses. Infections set in. Digestive problems come back. In Mike's current state, even the smallest setback could wipe out any gains, or do even worse. In mid-February, things seemed to be OK. By early March, the small cracks in his already fragile health began to deepen.

Oddly, everyone was seeing this but me. I clung so desperately to the things that I thought were good news that I wouldn't accept anything that would contradict them. Where most saw the end coming, I saw a temporary setback.

Around that time I had some business to attend to back in Oklahoma City. I spent the evening before with Mike, telling him I had to go home for a few days, but I'd be back. The next morning, I packed up my car and started driving south on Interstate 25.

My wife stayed in Denver, and it was she who called me when I was somewhere just north of Pueblo in southern Colorado.

"You need to come back," she said. "This is happening. This is happening now."

By "happening," she meant that Mike had decided, with certainty, that he was done fighting. He'd spoken with his doctors, asking the questions that mattered most. If he continued, what would his life be like? Would he be bed-ridden at home for the remainder of his days? Would he even leave the hospital? The outlook was grim: He'd probably never work again. His eyesight would never recover. If was able to leave the hospital at all, he'd likely be confined to a bed at home, unable to spend time outside (the sun's rays aggravate GVH), and that in all likelihood, he'd be back in the hospital in short order anyway. Realistically, it was doubtful he'd ever leave the hospital at all, his new home becoming the ward he was on, one in which few people ever left alive. For those who did, their lives outside those walls were painful and short. After hearing what they had to say, he decided he'd rather face death than continue a blind, medicated, painful and fruitless existence.

The next few days, all the family gathered. Friends from Mike's office and his church dropped by. By now, he was heavily drugged and only occasionally lucid. During one of those times, a pastor and a friend dropped in, and Mike offered them one last piece of advice, telling them "Love God, love people," before slipping back into a state of medicated Neverland.

Mike's last day was the most horrible thing I've ever witnessed. Heavy doses of drugs had taken over, but his GVH was completely unimpeded in its quest to eat his body from the inside out. At one point, he vomited violently, painfully, a bloody last bit of agony before drifting back into the pharmaceutical haze of pain meds. The hours dragged on, his breathing slowed. Afternoon turned to night. Slow breathing became shallow. Exhales were awful groans; we had no idea if the sounds he was making reflected pain, fear, or if they were mere unconscious physical reactions to the air passing over his vocal chords. Nevertheless, each one hit us like a hammer.

We told him that we loved him. That he didn't have to suffer anymore. That it was OK to let go.

In the pre-dawn hours of March 23, 2011, his breathing stopped. Mike was gone.

Doctors told us that most people with Stage Four GVH don't make it more than a couple of weeks. Mike fought it for more than four months.

****

Seventeen months after Mike passed, I was at the east ridge trailhead of Quandary Peak. My brother Steve was there, along with his wife and three kids. Also along for the ride was my oldest niece Liz, who had become exceptionally close to Mike in recent years.

We were there for a family reunion, and that morning, this was the crew that wished to see what the peak was like.

The day was beautiful, the skies blue. We hiked together for most of the route before splitting into a couple of groups. We took in the views from the ridge, spied the ever-present mountain goats, then made the last push up the ridge till you get to a one-hundred-yard flat stretch right before the summit. I watched as Liz, my niece Hillary and her brother Hunter took the honors of summiting first, then waited as Steve, his wife Beth and daughter Hannah topped out a couple of minutes later.

I drank in their summit experience – taking crazy pictures, getting a bite to eat, reliving the funny moments and the tough parts. I told them that the mountain they'd chosen that day was Mike's favorite. It felt good to be there with them.

On my second ascent of Quandary Peak I understood why Mike enjoyed that mountain so much.

EIGHT: FAITH

*"Now faith is being sure of what we hope for and
certain of what we do not see."*

– Hebrews 11:1

I've heard a lot of people say that when they want to
go to church, they go outside. Being in nature and
admiring creation is just as meaningful as showing up
to Sunday morning services, or so the narrative goes.

Some might contend this is an excuse to avoid
church, and that might have been the conclusion I
would have made many years ago, back when life
was a little simpler, more black-and-white, a neater,
tidier version than what it's become. It's different
now. Life can get seismic, and a lot can change when
the ground shakes hard enough.

In the times where I've been a regular at church, I've
learned plenty and come to know a number of really
good people. I felt the power of a good service, those
times when you feel like God is there with you. That
hasn't been a common experience for me; I usually
walk away from a Sunday service having learned

something positive or insightful and spent a few hours that morning with people I care about. But there are other times when I've felt God move. These have been rare moments for me. But they're indelible.

So let's circle back to that "church of the outdoors" thing. Like I said, I might have scoffed at the idea before, but then something happened deep inside the high country woodlands of the Carson National Forest of northern New Mexico years ago.

I've mentioned Wheeler Peak a few times. My first visit there, in 2002, had me hiking a short distance on its lower flanks. A year later, I was back with my brother Mike and my friend Rick.

Rick and I drove to Red River to meet up with Mike, who'd trekked south from Denver. The trip was my idea, but Mike was the real mountain expert. Rick and I were along for the ride.

We hiked the peak's East Fork Trail, the longest route to the top at more than twenty-one miles round trip. We were all in good shape, packed light and kept a great pace gaining the 3,500 feet to the summit in good time. We took lots of pictures, munched on trail food and high-fived each other upon topping out. We hung out just long enough to see the clouds beginning to gather, then started back down.

The skies went gray as storm clouds moved in. Passing by Horseshoe Lake and getting below treeline, we continued a fast pace to avoid any possible lightning hazards.

Down we went, through a seemingly endless stretch of woods. We joked a lot, razzing each other about our alpine farts and wanting to make sure we weren't behind the most frequent violator, which of course was Mike. Not that it did any good. He was a faster hiker than Rick and I. He'd rip one, we'd groan about it, and he'd just laugh. Juvenile humor helps pass the time.

That only lasted so long. Hike enough hours, expend enough energy, and fatigue takes over. Conversation stops. All you can do is concentrate on putting one foot in front of the other and look for landmarks that let you know you're getting closer to the end. Seven hours into it, we took a break, peeling off our packs and tossing our hiking poles to the side. And then we sat down, perching atop a rock or a log with a weary thud.

The silence continued, but it was anything but uncomfortable. A light rain had begun to fall about an hour earlier, a steady thing slightly harder than a drizzle. Thunder rumbled in the distance – powerful, lasting and, in a strange way, comforting. The southern Rockies had been pretty dry at that time, so the rains were more than just a relief – they were a signal for the woods to come alive. If you've never smelled the aroma of a dry alpine forest when it gets a badly needed rain, well, all I can tell you is it's one of the sweetest things that will ever fill your nose.

It occurred to me what I was seeing, hearing and smelling was probably the same thing pre-Columbian peoples saw, heard and smelled centuries ago. For that matter, the day's scene was a reprise of natural events going back eons. And here we were, reliving natural history, ages upon ages later. When you think about how short our lives are in comparison to the world in which we live, it makes you feel small.

I dwelled on that thought, how tiny I was in this grand place. I thought about how the mountains themselves were life-giving things, storing up water from winter snows, or summer rains like the one we were in, feeding small trickles which became creeks and streams, gathering themselves to become mighty rivers, feeding the world's oceans with fresh water, nourishing the seas which in turn would give birth to clouds that would travel across the waters and over land, stopping at the high peaks to begin the cycle all over again. Such a beautiful system, one in which any missing piece might undo the whole thing.

Those mountains, nature's water towers, are created from immense power. Tectonic forces born deep inside the Earth's eternally stoked furnace push vast masses of rock skyward over millions of years, or in the case of volcanoes, many years less. Water and gravity eventually tear the mightiest peaks down, but somewhere else, replacements are being built, centimeters at a time, over untold millions of years more. The earth's constantly changing face keeps us alive, and doing so is an exercise in perfect patience, one we humans can barely detect but are ultimately dependent.

Again, smallness.

Of course, the earth would be a floating cloud of dust if not for the sun, that burning ball of gasses some ninety-three million miles away. If you want a glimpse of how powerful it is, just consider that number: ninety-three million. As in miles. Yet, while so far away, looking right at it without peering through a tinted lens can injure your eyes. The sun powers our weather and makes the green things grow, among other things. If it were just a little closer, or a little farther away, what would we be? A burned up husk of stone, or a frozen wasteland of rock and ice, which would, in either case, likely make Earth lifeless.

The same could be said if it were much bigger or smaller, or something other than what it is now. So many things have to be just right for us to even exist.

And yet here we are. We look at the continuance of life as inevitable because we've never known a future or a past where that wasn't true. Cosmically speaking, it's rather fragile and fleeting.

The thunder boomed from the distance again as small rain drops bounced off thirsty pine needles, bare rock and my sweaty head, reinforcing that idea of smallness. All I really am is a bag of carbon and water, with some other elements mixed in. Yet here I am on this trail, electrical impulses flowing throughout my body giving me not only life, but the ability to contemplate the nature of the universe.

Have you ever thought about how miraculous it is that you wake up every day and breathe? How your heart keeps beating, asleep or awake, without you having to tell it to do so? How the tiny bit of electricity, charging through your nerves, knows exactly how to move your muscles so you can stand, walk, or run? Yeah, we are small. Really small. But life is an incredible, big thing.

I suppose these are the thoughts that race through your mind when you're in a beautiful place, your energy spent from a day's worth of exertion. There's nothing but silence around you, save the sounds of the storm, the wind in the trees, and the steady rush of waters flowing downhill in an unseen creek below.

No fart jokes here. Just contemplation. Meditative, quiet contemplation.

And then the next feeling came up on me, welling up like a slow-rising tide: gratitude. At that moment, I was grateful to be there, happy to hear the Earth speak, happy to be able to get up that morning and hike to the top of a high mountain.

Sitting on the side of the trail, I was grateful. Grateful to God. And I worshipped.

****

Some of my Christian friends who read this won't be happy with the whole "millions of years" references I threw out there, though most will probably be OK with it. There will likely be more folks who will shake their heads at the religious overtones. Not everyone believes in God, or perhaps they believe, but not in the way that I do. And that's OK. I learned a long time ago that there is no way to make everyone happy when the topic of faith comes up.

I've also learned that there are plenty of barriers between people and God, and that many of these obstacles are man-made. It's going to be different in other countries than it is here in the U.S., but what bothers lots of people is how some people of faith behave.

I wish I had a buck for every time someone complained to me that the reason they don't go to church is because of all the hypocrites there. Well, I've got news for you. There are hypocrites everywhere, of all faiths and non-faiths. Hypocrisy is a human condition. Want to see a hypocrite? Go take a walk outside where people are. You're welcome.

Hell, I'm guilty of it. It's not hard to imagine. Have I made an absolute statement of something I think is right, or maybe wrong, and then proceeded to do something that contradicts that very statement? Yep. It's happened. Nothing to brag about, and certainly not something of which I want to make a habit or see emulated. But it's happened. I'm sure it's happened to all of us.

But I understand how reluctant people might be to test the waters of faith, given what they see every day. I've often worried for the church when I see a huge block of it falling in lockstep with a political party. That might be fine if you're really into that party, but disconcerting if you're not.

And I've been long perplexed at the preoccupation so many have with a couple of very narrow issues that don't affect them much, if at all, while turning a blind eye to other problems that affect so many. We'll sermonize about the minutest details of people's personal lives and latch on to wedge issues like a pride of lions feasting on a fallen wildebeest, but passively shrug when it comes to how we should treat the poor, the sick, the marginalized and the oppressed. It seems our moral appetites favor the ease of telling others what to do and shun the hard tasks that take time, effort and resources we'd rather keep for ourselves.

Perhaps this is an example of why there is such a steady decline in organized religion. Another: a strong perception by those "outside the fold" that those who don't look, speak and act right are not just undesirable, but a threat. Some of the biggest names in our religious hierarchy nod approvingly at unsavory characters who make the proper promises, but slam the door shut on foreign-speaking refugees fleeing poverty, persecution, war and terrorism.

Maybe this is why some people avoid religion altogether. I get that, but I go back to the hypocrisy example – these types of behaviors are not unique to the religious or anyone else. It's part of our DNA, and the church itself is made of people. I don't like it either, but I also realize it's the reality of living in a world filled with humans. I try not to let that get in the way of how I see God.

But here comes the kicker. I have definitely found myself challenged with reconciling some of the things that have happened to me and to those I care about with a belief that there is a God up there who is looking out for us.

More specifically, I'm stumped about why things went down the way they did with Mike.

I don't want to sound childlike when it comes to losing a loved one, specifically when that person dies before his or her time. I know these things happen. People get sick, they get in car accidents, they even get killed at the hands of others or by their own hand.

Almost every death on this planet is a tragedy to someone. The sense of loss is deep. When you think about it in a clinical way, it's kind of strange – everyone dies. It's just as common (and with an equal emotional pull) as childbirth. It's safe to say that we have not evolved past the point of grieving death, and that's a good thing. We're not robots with batteries that go dead. We're living souls who breathe, love, learn and give. Any time something like that is lost is an occasion to mourn.

The trouble I have with Mike's death is two-fold. The first deals with how he died. Death by GVH is nothing less than torture as the body attacks itself in such a painful, comprehensive and relentless way. Day after day, nothing but agony on your skin, in your gut, and just about everywhere else. You lose all privacy – and dignity – as the bedpan becomes your default restroom, and someone always has to be there to clean you up. You lose your vision. Your strength to walk. The ability to eat real food.

While in the hospital, your room becomes your prison, never changing, no escape. And you never get any real sleep, at least not anything more than a couple of hours at a time. Either the sickness gets you or you're awakened by nurses who run tests and administer medications day and night.

This goes on and on without any real relief. Every day it's the same awful routines with only a couple of momentary patches of relief. If you don't recover, really recover, from GVH, this is the type of life you'll have until your last days. It's no wonder most people who experience the worst of this only make it a couple of weeks. The mindless cruelty of the condition left me shaken.

The second problem I have is the waste of it all. At forty-seven, Mike seemed to have a lot of life ahead of him. A wife, a son and a daughter. Mike was the main provider for his family, financially speaking, and they'd carved out a good life for themselves.

I'd mentioned how Mike had his own crisis of belief, and how he emerged from that time a stronger and wiser person. It affected him deeply, and changed the way he looked at people. Mike was a kind and generous guy, accepting people where they were, but always trying to find a way to make others' lives a little brighter. It didn't matter who it was – total strangers, best friends, his kids, me – it seemed he had the right piece of wisdom or encouragement for anyone he met.

In Mike, there was so much potential for good. Not just for himself or his family, but for everyone. The Bible talks about being "salt and light" in the world, an ancient reference that can be summed up by the qualities possessed by those things: the ability to purify and preserve, and the quality of revealing the world as it really is. This is a thing Christians aspire to be. Mike went beyond that. He lived it. Mike was salt and light.

The energy, passion and intensity Mike had for how he should live his life guaranteed that he lived very intentionally: Every day for Mike was an opportunity to make a difference. Few people are like this, and yet it's clear that what this world needs are more people who do just as Mike did.

So in the hours and days and weeks and months after Mike died – even now, to be honest – I have what has so far been the unanswerable question:

Why waste a life like this?

I remember a conversation I had with my dad shortly after Mike died. As you might expect, he was crushed. Any parent would be. I cannot imagine the devastation of having to watch your child die, attend his funeral, and then live the rest of your days without the person to whom you helped give life, raise and see become a man.

We were at the church where his memorial services were being held, a big place in suburban Denver where Mike and his family worshipped regularly. Several hundred people were there to pay their respects.

"All I can say is this better have some purpose to it," my dad told me, staring off at no place in particular. He looked tired and beaten. "There has to be some greater good."

"There is," I reassured him, trying to take up the role of spiritual counselor. "We may not know what it is, and it may be awhile before we see it. But it will reveal itself."

At the time, I think I believed it. I sure wanted to. I had to believe somehow, some way, God would use this for some amazingly triumphant work of good, and it would be plain to anyone with eyes and ears that a grand plan was at work and would end with a beautiful flourish. But as weeks turned into months, and then years, all I see is hurt. Every birthday that passes, every holiday, every anniversary of his death brings back the reality that Mike is gone and he's not coming back. And I have yet to see this grand plan manifesting itself, no divine ray of light coming forth from a tomb explaining why Mike had to die, and why he had to suffer so. It makes me wonder if what I told my dad was just to comfort him, if I really believed it, and if not, whether that made me a liar. Perhaps my dad knew I was just trying to be reassuring. But still…

So I put out a lot of angry prayers asking why. That may sound cliché, but it's the truth. Those were honest prayers that seemed to be answered by silence. It's a maddening quiet leaving me feeling that much more accusatory, much in the way Job did, I suppose. And that brings up some interesting questions. Bear with me here.

What if I could have a face-to-face with God about this subject? Might he be able to throw a few things back at me? I can recall days where I seemed like a good man, saying and doing all the right things, at least by most people's standards. But there have been other times when that has not been the case. I possess a long list of images of things I've done that aren't all that flattering, things of which there is no defense. I'm equal parts sinner as saint, with plenty of Sunday School gold stars to go around, but a track record of breaking just about all those biblical commandments, one by one, leaving behind a selfish wake of shame and hurt.

So there you have it: Me, with a legitimate gripe about what I see as a grave injustice, but without a moral leg to stand on. It's a hell of a crossroads, and that's where I find myself: Stuck in a standoff with God.

****

I haven't always been a "religious" person. Growing up, we didn't go to church much. To my parents' credit, we were raised right, and I can recall believing in God from an early age. When I was 10, I went to a summer Bible school program where I learned a sliver of scripture I can still remember, Psalm 34:8. I can still recite it word for word, decades later. But faith and God weren't things that I took seriously until I became a teenager. Something clicked then, and it has stuck with me since, the idea of treating others as you would like to be treated, loving people as much as yourself, loving God, and if everyone did these things, how much better the world would be. I've devoted a considerable amount of time reading and studying the Bible, trying to learn what I could about God, and how our lives are supposed to be.

Funny thing about faith: It's really easy to believe when things are going well. A full belly, a healthy body, a roof overhead, a couple of cars in the driveway and plenty of money in the bank have a way of making you feel "blessed," something that is reinforced if you also believe you are a good person who can generally be trusted to do the right thing. You might be surprised to know that there are quite a few of these people, at least in this country, anyway.

But faith becomes hard when things don't go well. It gets even more difficult when you believe you've done all the right things, and yet you still suffer. It's compounded when you witness injustices, or when you become a victim of those injustices. Combine all those things with a significant tragedy, and a life of faith becomes an existential struggle. In short, you can become quite lost.

Back in my favorite trail running spot, I spent a lot of time exploring about forty-five miles or so of trails that wind their way over a few ridges and throughout an old forest. In the course of that exploration, I got lost a lot. It's not like getting lost in, say, Montana's Bob Marshall Wilderness, but it's easy to get turned around, disoriented and stuck in a place where you might run out of daylight before you run out of trail. So that could be a problem.

But I discovered something about that place: the ridges run from north to south, and they are parallel to the Arkansas River. It makes it really easy to figure out which direction you're headed. So if I ever got off-route to the point of fruitless bushwhacking, I knew that if all clse failed I could casily figure out which way was south, and then start moving that way. Eventually, going south will lead you back to the trailhead.

Remembering this trick has helped me quite a bit on that trail system. Recalling those landmarks – the geological features that run north-to-south – is a sure-fire way to get un-lost.

That's a little bit how faith has worked out for me. Strangely, even with the level of disillusionment with which I was saddled after Mike's death, and the increasing cynicism that's grown in me about "the church" of late, I still get reminders from my past, the moments that led me to believe in the first place, and the lessons I've learned since. I think back to those deeper thoughts on the trails of Wheeler Peak, and how the improbability of it all seems to be reconciled by the existence of a creator. There are times when I wanted to chuck it all, call myself an agnostic and walk away like a blackjack dealer going on break. The trouble is, I always end up walking away… south.

I'm sure it's not this way for everyone, but there are times when I'm out in a wilderness area, perhaps approaching a dramatic peak, or maybe when I stop to check out the view from a tall summit and I can't help but feel gratitude toward God about what I'm seeing. I have a video I made from one of those summits, shot while I was alone atop Colorado's Missouri Mountain on a cloudy, sketchy fall day when the weather looked as if it could turn for the worse at any moment. Autumn colors were showing themselves on lower slopes of the Sawatch Range, mixed in with the deep green spruces and pines, then lighter greens and yellows of alpine willows, and finally, higher up, tundra and bare rock layered just so. The way the clouds swirled, combined with the vibrant colors of the basin below, made me feel as if I needed to thank someone for what I was looking at, to show some appreciation for the ability to even hike up to that mountaintop. Lots of people can't, or won't, and they miss out on one of life's most wonderful displays: the visuals atop the world's high places. I could have said, "Wow!" or "Rad!" or something like that, but instead, I blurted out, "To God be the glory!" And it felt right.

If you're reading this as a person who believes in God, you get it. If, on the other hand, you don't know if there's a God or don't believe at all, this is a harder thing to explain. Your rational self will likely file it away as superstition, a philosophical crutch, or a stubbornly comfortable tradition. I understand that. But if you really want to understand what's going on in the head of someone like me, one who believes and yet struggles with that belief, you have to go deeper.

What I've come to see, in basic terms, goes something like this:

God is big, impossibly so. Big enough to stoke the fires of the sun, to write the laws of physics, and to set the universe in motion by saying, "BANG!" and then it happens with immeasurable force. This same God is also interested and invested in the smaller things, to the point of knowing the number of hairs on your head. He's fathomless, yet knowable. The harshest of judges, yet ultimately merciful, compassionate and caring. He's unseen, yet his handiwork is everywhere. Physically inaudible, but when you hear him "speak," it's clear. He's mysterious. And from my own experiences, a paraphrase of C.S. Lewis seems to ring particularly true: God is not safe. But he is good.

And with that realization, that childhood Bible verse – my ridgeline pointing me south – comes back to me: "Oh taste and see that the Lord is good; blessed is the man that trusts in him."

NINE: WILDERNESS

"Wilderness is not only a haven for native plants and animals but it is also a refuge from society. It's a place to go to hear the wind and little else, see the stars and the galaxies, smell the pine trees, feel the cold water, touch the sky and the ground at the same time, listen to coyotes, eat the fresh snow, walk across the desert sands, and realize why it's good to go outside of the city and the suburbs."
– John Muir

Caught in an early summer deluge, there was no way what I was experiencing could be considered fun. It had been raining steadily for a couple of hours, sometimes torrentially, and I was waterlogged and far from shelter. My allegedly waterproof boots were soaked through, as was anything else connected to me. There were another couple miles of rugged hiking between me and the car, and the threat of lightning loomed. Most worrisome to me were the creek crossings. They were all dry this time of year, but the rains were heavy enough that I had to think about flash flooding should the storms continue to rage.

And those were the least of my problems. At that time, just a few years ago, my life was heading down the shitter at a sprinter's pace. Personal life, career, you name it – everything looked grim, driven to new levels of dysfunction for someone who was used to having his act together.

It would have been easy to dwell on those circumstances, and the fact that the trail up the hill was pretty much a flowing river, had I not stopped to take a look around. In the low drone of rainfall and distant peals of thunder, this place I'd come to know on many other hikes and climbs looked far different.

The Wichita Mountains of southwestern Oklahoma are among the most ancient peaks in the world, more than 500 million years by some estimates. Wind, water and time have eroded them to what they are today, rounded humps and jagged ridges of granite abruptly interrupting the prairie that dominates the western half of the state. They are an oasis of verticality in a desert of flatness, mountains that would be mere foothills in nearly every other Western state, a semi-arid haunt for elk, deer and buffalo. Hikers, rock climbers and wildlife enthusiasts are drawn to the Wichitas from all over Oklahoma and north Texas, mostly because the landscape is so much different from anything else for hundreds of miles. They're also a protected federal wildlife refuge, making them one of the few expanses of public lands in Oklahoma. To my friends, I say the Wichitas are "my Oklahoma happy place."

But blurred by the steady rains, they just looked different. The reds, browns and pinks of the sun-drenched granite were turned into a shade of gray slightly darker than the skies, and the distant peaks, easily distinguished under clear conditions, now formed a steely, jagged and unified skyline resembling the spine of a dragon's back. Indeed, if not for the warmth of the air, one might have looked at the scene and thought it something out of the fjords of Norway or some other distant, frigid and alien land. The sight halted my march for a few moments, transfixing me with a magical pull that made me oblivious to the assault of raindrops permeating my clothes.

For those few moments, where I was engulfed in the wilderness, something was speaking to me.

"Stop," it was saying. *"Stop what you're doing. Stop and listen."*

Call it an inner voice, a whisper from God, or whatever suits you, but the message was clear. I had strolled into a wilderness and, in doing so, walked into a storm. The reality of my surroundings was a metaphor of my life, and a sign of things to come. As bad as things seemed to be, they were only going to get worse, what with the pending job loss and Mike's passing. During that time, I was going to need something calm, steady and ever-present just to help me keep my bearings.

"Stop and listen," the voice repeated. *"You're going to need me. You need me right now. You don't know how much, but I can tell you that I've been trying to say this to you for some time. I hope I have your attention. Stop and listen."*

And so I did.

Like so many times before, I had gone outside that day, unsure what to expect, hoping to experience or learn something new, but never fully knowing it would mean so much more now, that this would be what I needed to weather the tempest to come. When all else failed, I did what I'd done often before, in better times.

I walked in wilderness.

****

The concept of wilderness has a different meaning now than it once did. When we think of it today, we envision wild places, protected from the hands of people, set aside for wildlife. Conservation comes to mind. A wilderness is a place to explore, maybe somewhere to go backpacking or camping or take photographs of animals and landscapes. There is a sense of mystery, risk and even danger when people think about wilderness, but for the most part, the vibe is neutral, neither good nor evil.

But it wasn't always this way.

It's only recently that we've been able to tame landscapes by road and rail, or bypass them entirely by air. Much of what was wild, unexplored country is now cleared for farms, ranches and communities. Before those days, wilderness had an entirely different feel.

Wilderness was scary and dark. Entire mythologies have been created in people's minds, legends of things that go bump in the night, trying to explain the noises created by creatures and spirits unseen. When people were punished just short of execution, they were exiled, sentenced to walk into the wild with the idea that they would eventually meet a terrifying, painful and lonely death in savage lands beyond the walls of civilization.

Try to put yourself in that scenario, where you're given a few days' worth of food and the clothes on your back and told to go, forever, into an impenetrable wood or a vast desert filled with unknown dangers from hungry predators you won't see until it's too late, or won't hear until an entire pack of them sets upon you. Suddenly wilderness isn't peaceful or fascinating. It's frightening.

I think about this every time I drive through the Midwest, an unending sea of rolling countryside that ends abruptly with the appearance of the Rocky Mountains. I cannot imagine what the pioneers thought when they first saw that range, having endured the harshness of the Great Plains only to be confronted by an ancient wall of rock that blocked their route west for hundreds of miles to the north and the south. If you were in that group, you'd already come so far as to make turning back unimaginable, but going forward would lead to an entirely new set of problems. And when they were in the folds of those mountains, with greater and deadlier challenges all around, can you imagine the creeping feeling of despair that would overcome you at the first sign of a big snow? Some made it to California to try their hand at panning for gold. Others ended up like the Donner Party, reduced to hypothermia, starvation and cannibalism while stuck at a high pass during a deadly Sierra blizzard.

That's what wilderness was back then, and still is now to a large degree, modern perceptions aside. But still, back then and today, people go. They'll leave the comforts or familiarity of home and point themselves down a trail into the unknown. Their motivations are diverse. A lot of the people I know seek out wilderness to calm their minds or to see something beautiful amid peace and quiet. Other people head into wild areas because they don't fit in anywhere else, or perhaps they're running from something. In that respect, things haven't changed much.

So there it is. Wilderness can be a place of refuge or banishment, a barrier to a dream or perhaps a dream in itself. I'd like to think that anyone could go into the wilderness and come back changed for the better, similar to what we saw with the likes of John Muir. Muir was happy out there, in his element, and the writings of his explorations in the Sierras have made this country a better place. But I also know some people are forced to go, by either their life circumstances, or perhaps something more inside their head. They go to escape, like refugees fleeing their burning town, the wreckage of their lives irretrievably lost, and their future in the wild uncertain.

Whatever the case, wilderness has a few constants. Its rules are as old as time itself, and they are not flexible. Wilderness may be traversed, explored, mapped and named, but it is untamed. Those who go into that realm can find lessons, blessings, sanctuary and transformation, but they can also find injury, tragedy, sickness and death. It partially depends on how ready you are for such things, but also random chance. Wilderness is indifferent to your presence, and when you happen to get in the way of its natural flow, great woes can unfold. That's what makes it dangerous.

****

I originally planned to camp overnight at an improved campsite maintained by the U.S. Fish and Wildlife Service, but I got too lazy to get my gear together the night before. So I decided to do a day trip instead. The Wichita Mountains were about two-and-a-half hours away from my house, so if I left before dawn I'd get there by mid-morning, hike to Sunset Peak, top out, and head home well before dark.

I figured it would be hot, and I prepared for that, but in failing to take advantage of the wonderful tools of modern weather prediction (I didn't bother to check the day's forecast), I headed out the door without a clue as to what was barreling in from the west – a historic squall line of storms destined to dump record amounts of rain across western Oklahoma. I walked outside, saw clouds, and figured I'd get a break from the early June sun, and that maybe this day hike would be more pleasant than I thought. Little did I know.

A couple of hours later, I checked in at the visitor center, drove to the trailhead and popped my pack on my back. There were a few other people hiking on the trails close to the trailhead, but they looked like they were on their way out, saying something about seeing a buffalo up the trail and not liking the looks of the skies.

I figured I was good at tackling whatever the elements threw my way. I'd seen plenty of buffalo before without ever feeling like I was in any real danger. *Let the noobs scurry for cover. I'm heading out.*

So I hiked on for about twenty minutes, and then the rain started. At first, it wasn't too bad. I put on a light rain jacket, made sure my camera was stowed in a dry place and continued. But the rain kept coming down harder, and then I heard it: booming thunder that closely followed a flash from the skies.

The rain intensified, accompanied by increasingly frequent lightning and thunder. At the time, I was on a trail through a grove thick with scrub oak and cedar, but most of the area I planned to hike was far more open, going over rocky high points with no cover at all. Sunset Peak was just such a place, bare and exposed to the dangers barreling down from the storm above. There wasn't going to be any summit that day.

Twenty minutes into this thing, and I was forced to contemplate bagging it and going home. That seemed unacceptable. At the same time, lightning wasn't something to just brush off, so I hunkered down in a thick stand of trees to wait it out. Surely whatever line of storms was overhead would pass, and things would be safer.

I sat there, listening to the thunder rumble across the sky and the rain as it pelted the ground and the leaves. Being so still made me aware of how little I could hear of anything except for the rain. After a few minutes, it appeared to abate – the thunder seemed more distant, and the rain slacked off to where I figured it was OK to be on my way again. Maybe the day could be salvaged after all.

I was encouraged. I had a bit of a spring in my step, and the storm was extra spice to a day that would hopefully distract me from the troubles back home.

I never saw it coming.

The woods were thick, and my eyes were focused on an opening in the path where the trail crossed a creek bed, then went up a ridge and over to a valley that could conceivably take me to either Sunset Peak (yeah, I was still thinking about doing that) or maybe another, less committing destination.

But first, a loud, bovine snort. And then, a blurry flash of black out of the corner of my eye. I jumped to the side, let out a muted "Whoa!" and felt something big – really big – breeze by me. Wheeling around, I saw the buffalo sprint up the trail, stop and turn to face me from about fifty feet away. I just gazed at it, my body not quite comprehending the situation before the adrenaline began to flow.

The buffalo, it would seem, had the same idea that I had, taking cover in the woods during the relentless downpour. The foliage from the trees and the underbrush was so thick that I didn't even see it, and given the noise from the rain, I'm not sure the beast knew I was coming until I was right on top of it. I startled it, prompting it to burst out of the undergrowth, and I managed to sidestep what might have been a life-threatening disaster with no one around to help. To this day, I'm dumbfounded as to how I failed to spot it, and further amazed that I didn't end up gored or trampled, or maybe both. The buffalo stood its ground down the trail, leaving my path forward clear. I backed away slowly as the buffalo stared me down, unmoving. Clearing the trees and out of sight from my furry friend, my heart kept pounding, just a little faster, as the adrenaline dump ensued.

That was a close one. I turned back up the trail, took a look at the leaden skies and marched up the next hill.

****

John Krakauer wrote a book in the 1990s about a young man named Chris McCandless, a recent college grad who saw where his life was headed and chose the opposite way. Instead of taking a job and chasing the American Dream, he donated or abandoned most of his possessions and hitchhiked his way across the West until finally achieving his dream of reaching Alaska for a summer of living alone in the bush.

He died out there, starving to death from a tragic confluence of high waters of a nearby river cutting off his exit and eating plants that chemically set his body on a landslide of escalating malnutrition. A lot of Alaskans scoff at the posthumous fame McCandless received (many admirers of his story make the pilgrimage to the bus-turned-hunter's cabin where his remains were found), deriding him as a novice who stupidly attempted an adventure of which he was woefully unqualified.

To an extent, these armchair critics might be right, and I think some people's veneration of the guy may be somewhat misplaced. But summing up McCandless's life by the months and weeks leading to his death is unfair. Before he set foot on the Stampede Trail, McCandless – who was utterly lost in the "normal" world – found himself on the road, on the trail, and in wilderness.

Krakauer did a thorough job reporting McCandless's story, talking to a great number of people who knew him, be they family or the friends he made during his travels. Letters, notes and journal entries filled in much of the rest. But can you imagine what

McCandless might have been able to say had he been able to hike out of his camp and back into civilization? Just think of all the observations he'd gathered over the years he was on the road, recollections of people he befriended. What lessons might he have shared? Is it possible he could have reconciled a past he despised with the experiences he underwent? How much did he grow? Did he find peace out there?

Sadly, we'll never know.

One of his contemporaries, however, walked into the wild and survived it.

Cheryl Strayed fled a life spiraling out of control and set out to hike the Pacific Crest Trail around the time McCandless met his end. Her time on the trail – traversing deserts, forests, snowfields and more – included its fair share of mishaps, happy gatherings, interesting people and a couple of close scrapes.

As she wrote in her book *Wild*, all that time alone in the wilderness was exactly what she needed. She exiled a few demons, kicked a nagging drug habit and found a way to come to terms with the untimely death of her mother. Wilderness wasn't solely responsible for her healing, and I'd never tell anyone that a lengthy stay in the wild is guaranteed to bring some sort of spiritual tonic to cure life's ills. But it was the medium that stoked McCandless's fire and freed the young Strayed from the jail cell that her life had become. Certainly, McCandless's time in the wild made his life bigger than it had been before, and Strayed – now a famous author – can look back at her trek more than two decades ago and point to that as her life's turning point.

I wish I could put my finger on what it is about the backcountry that does this for people. It's not for everyone, but a lot of us get an almost medicinal benefit from hitting the trail, be it for a couple of days or a few years. If I were to guess, it would be this: a combination of visceral, heart-pumping experiences, beautiful sights, smells and sounds, and moments of quiet that allow our brains to process loads of information without being distracted by the next task, obligation or crisis that so often populate what would (should?) be otherwise peaceful, empty spaces in time.

Quiet moments are often times when the light comes on. If you're a praying person, long, heartfelt and brutally honest inquiries of God are made then. Sometimes there's an answer. Sometimes there's just quiet. Sometimes, quiet is all you need.

****

Not long after I left Mr. Buffalo in my rearview mirror, I reached a fork in the trail. The rain had calmed to a light drizzle, though I was still hearing a little thunder. The trail split off, with one track heading west toward Sunset Peak a couple of miles away, and another continuing south toward a familiar landmark called Crab Eyes. I'd been to Crab Eyes a couple of times before, and even climbed it once. It's one of the few places I don't mind returning to again and again.

My time out there was getting a little long, with all those weather delays and wildlife encounters. Unsure what the skies might bring, it was then that I had to admit that exploring Sunset Peak would have to wait for another day. So Crab Eyes it was.

As you might imagine, the formation gets its name from its appearance. It's a minor peak in the Wichitas, made up of a broad fin of granite that rises abruptly from the ground that has two similar-sized boulders perched on top. When you look upon it, it has all the appearance of a giant, stony hermit crab.

On a more aesthetic level, Crab Eyes carries an almost spiritual weight. It sits smack in the middle of a wilderness area, with views of almost every peak in the range. Hiking to it has a feel like you're treading into a throne room, and as you ascend to its headwall that aura is confirmed – the tall wall of rock serving as a foundation to the giant slabs holding the crab's eyes aloft, looming over you as if to let you know your small place in this great, big realm. When you get to the top of that headwall and look around, commanding views of the surrounding hills and peaks abound. If not a seat of power, the Crab Eyes formation could be a temple, with the base of the eyes the perfect spot for an altar. That might sound melodramatic until you see it for yourself. The

Wichitas are sacred ground to the Kiowa tribe for a reason.

Getting to the top of Crab Eyes is done one of two ways. You hike up to the north ridge, then shimmy up between two tight granite slabs before reaching the upper part of the ridge just below the eyes. The ridge is split, leaving you with the option of either awkwardly crab-walking (no pun intended) to the top with your hands on one slab and your feet on the other, or you can simply do a tight-rope walk up one of the slabs. It's a gradual friction climb about two feet wide with a fifty-foot sheer drop to your left.

That's the "easy" way up.

The other way is to do a vertical crack climb that requires a good deal of skill and a willingness to shred your hands on the grippy, granite surface.

I'd done the easy route before, but not on that day. Instead, I decided that getting to the landmark was good enough, finding a flat, scenic overlook with great views of nearby Elk Mountain, Mount Lincoln and a number of other minor peaks.

The rain subsided and the lightning and thunder moved on. The sun was trying to break through the cloud bank – I could feel its warmth on my skin as I sat down and began to empty my pack of the food I'd brought. I snapped a few pictures and munched on a simple sandwich and some fruit. A full belly, the warming temps and the fatigue of the hike began to wash over me in a manner not unlike what you get after a big Thanksgiving dinner just before you let the TV play-by-play of a football game lull you to sleep. I stretched out on the rock, looking up at the sky: Still gray, but a lighter shade than what I'd seen when I first got there. Without the sound of the rain, thunder or wind, all I heard were bird songs.

I might compare that time in my life to something akin to a hurricane. Multiple crises started out as high winds before turning into a raging tempest, and then suddenly, things calmed. The gales tapered to a breeze and the rain quit altogether, and just for that moment, things were tranquil. I mean that on both the real and metaphorical level. More "life" storms were coming (my brother Mike getting sick, the loss of a job, and then Mike's death), but on this day, those problems were far away. And here in the wilderness, the storms that pounded me for the better part of a few hours had relented just long enough for me to lie back, prop my head on my pack and nap for about twenty minutes.

It had been months since I felt that kind of peace. Far away from anyone and all alone, in the belly of the wild, I felt safe.

****

It's important to note that as much as I like to get outside – as much as I *need* to get outside – I'm no Les Stroud or anything close to that. Hiking is awesome and camping is great. Some of the most memorable meals I've ever consumed have been around a campfire with friends, or even by myself at the top of a cliff with no one else around. But there are shows I like to watch, restaurants I frequent, and I sure do love my bed. All of these things go from fairly ordinary to top-shelf luxury when you've been eating dehydrated meals for a week, or sleeping on the ground in the cold for a few days too many, or stuck inside your cramped, stinky tent while a relentless storm soaks the skies for half a day. Les Stroud or John Muir wouldn't be bothered by such things. As for me, I'm the guy inhaling a bag of potato chips and a can of Coke at the first sign of a convenience store following a modest backpacking trip.

I suppose I'm a product of my environment, which is controlled and comfortable. And yet, for a number of reasons, it doesn't matter how much my back ached, how tired I got, how bad I smelled or how much I suffered – it won't be long before I'm itching to go out there again. It's part of the reason trail running appeals to me so much, as it gives me that mini-adventure, complete with a little pain and joy, before I have to head home, clean up and go to work or whatever. But that's just a temporary fix. As I'm writing this, I'm thinking of a dozen places I want to go, both close to home and far away, and wondering how I can make it happen? Who's going with me? How can I pull it off if I'm going solo?

I remember the bad times, the little sufferfests, and all of that. Those make for some good stories around the campfire or at a pub with friends. Even more than that, I remember those big moments.

I recall being blown away coming over Half Moon Pass in Colorado just as the early dawn light washed over a partially snow-covered Mount of the Holy Cross. It was one of the most breathtaking things I've ever seen.

There were the high-fives I shared with my brothers when Mike and I got Steve up his first 14er.

Or maybe that second trip up Mount Shavano.

My buddy Johnny and I did this one, traveling to Buena Vista, Colorado, to have a go at a modest snow climb up that mountain's Angel of Shavano couloir. Mike and I had hiked that peak five years before, but not via the Angel.

More importantly, it was also my first trip back to the Rockies since a rather ill-fated trip the year before, and the consequences of that one made me wonder if I'd ever enjoy a high summit again.

The story takes a little explaining. In July of 2008, I went on a trip to Thailand, and while exploring the wonderful beaches and cliffs of Railay Beach, I jumped off a small crag into some deeper water, with the idea of getting some air, splashing hard, then swimming a couple of hundred feet back to shore. No sweat, right?

Well, the waves were up, and so was the undercurrent. Added to that – I'm not the best swimmer in the world. So long story short, I almost drowned. Friends saw I was in trouble, swam out to meet me, and by the grace of God, I got back to shore safe and sound. Crisis averted, lesson learned.

Except that wasn't the end of it.

Whenever you aspirate sea water (which I did), it's very important that you go to a hospital (which I didn't). The body has a tough time getting that junk out of your lungs, so it just sits there, along with any microbes that might have been swimming in the sea before you welcomed them into your airway.

A few days later, a full-blown respiratory infection set in, and after a brief visit to the hospital back at home I was given some antibiotics and told I'd be OK. So I took the meds, and within a few days, I was feeling pretty good.

That was a good thing (so I thought) because I had plans to head to Colorado with some friends to hike up to the top of Mount Yale, elevation 14,196 feet. It was real touch-and-go for a few days after that near-drowning experience and the sickness that followed, but I felt good enough to make a go of it and hopefully make some memories with the fellas one more time before the summer ended.

Everything was going pretty well on that one, from the hike to camp to the first hour or so marching up Mount Yale's steep flanks.

The problem was whatever bug had nestled itself into my right lung a few weeks before wasn't gone. It had been knocked back – to the point where I felt well – but it was still there, just waiting to spring back to life. It did that somewhere between 12,000 and 13,000 feet, finally announcing itself in what felt like a side cramp. Winded and cramping, I caught up to a few of my buddies who had already topped out. But when it came time to go down, those side cramps – what I thought was a sign of poor conditioning – didn't go away. They persisted.

I wasn't sure what was going on – all I know is that I was freezing cold when I stopped (and the temperatures were within the upper 30s and low 40s, so not that cold) and cramped up when I got moving. And then, with rain clouds closing in and treeline still a couple of thousand feet below me, I had a nice hallucination. I thought I saw a friend taking a rest against a boulder, with his ballcap peeking out over the rock and his pack tossed to the side. I almost called out to him before I realized that the things I saw were just rocks.

This freaked me out a little bit, and I was worried about my condition. But I hadn't a clue how bad off I really was.

My condition, you see, was full-blown pneumonia. Added to that, there was also fluid building around the infected lung (which X-rays would show was 75 percent filled with gunk) as well as my heart, a triple-play that has been known to kill. (In a tragic coincidence, that was near the same time comedian Bernie Mac died from complications caused by similar maladies.) As an added bonus, the combination of the illness and the elevation gave me a nice case of altitude sickness.

Fortunately, I got off the mountain OK. Unfortunately, the recovery ended up peeling 18 pounds off my body and lasted more than two months. My doctor told me that I'd be fine, but that any future X-rays would show scarring in my right lung – a permanent reminder of my folly on Mount Yale.

I asked him whether getting that sick would put me at risk for recurrence if I decided to go skiing or climbing any other mountains. He said he didn't think it would, but in the back of my mind, I worried about it.

Nine months later, Johnny and I made our bid on Mount Shavano, a big but straightforward walkup peak not all that far from the scene of the previous year's debacle. Neither of us was in top shape, and this was the first time either of us had strapped on crampons and used an ice axe. We were the guys who bought a little courage at REI and marched into a new adventure with all the hubris and humor that comes with being a newbie.

The winds were blowing hard, coming over the saddle between Shavano and a nearby, lesser peak at a steady thirty-five miles per hour, gusting even higher and right into our faces. But we ambled our way up that skinny ribbon of snow to the saddle, then found one last, long stretch of snow to gain the summit.

Johnny got there first – he's always been a faster, better conditioned hiker than me. He turned down the slope, took out his camera and snapped a few shots of me kick-stepping those final few yards to the top. In one frame, I stopped, smiled, hoisted my ice axe into the air and let out a loud yell. I was tired, sore and gassed, and my back hurt like hell. I was wind- and sunburned. But so happy.

Nine months before, when I was stuck in bed enduring night sweats and feeling like absolute shit, I wondered if I'd ever see a mountaintop again. It was an irrational fear in hindsight, but real enough for me at the time. Gaining Shavano's summit months later I was so grateful I got another chance to do this.

And that's why I yelled that celebratory yell.

Now you know what I mean when I mention remembering the big moments.

****

The drizzle dampening my face at Crab Eyes let me know nap time was over. A lot of storm systems will move through an area in a single line while others march through in waves. The storm I was facing was the latter kind, raking its way across the plains in bands of heavy rain. Time to get moving.

The rain had been coming down hard enough that I feared the ground was getting saturated, and if any future downpour resembled what I saw that morning, flooding might become a risk. A speedy retreat to the trailhead seemed like a good idea.

When the rains came, they arrived with even more intensity than they had earlier that morning. The drizzle morphed into a steady rain, the drops getting bigger. Finally, the storm arrived in earnest, unloading everything it had. The trail itself had turned into a fast-flowing stream, even sporting small waterfalls in the steeper sections. Lightning and thunder returned. It wasn't an option to find some place to take shelter – no such place existed. I just had to push through.

There are a couple of ways you can look at that situation: bemoan the circumstances or brush it off. There was no way to stay dry, and those waterlogged boots sloshed underneath me, carrying who-knows-how-much extra weight. Being hopelessly wet is actually liberating, in that there isn't any point to finding a dry place to walk. It wasn't happening that day.

It is key to visualize how ridiculous this situation had become. I wasn't wading through the trail. The water wasn't deep. But I was definitely kicking up water with each footfall, audibly splashing along in some clumsy perversion of a Gene Kelley number without the benefit of dexterity, talent or an umbrella.

I'm ploddin' in the rain, just splashin' in the rain...

Yep, it was just that ridiculous.

The nature of things also made it slow going. It's hard to move fast when you're slipping on rocks and dragging boat-anchor-heavy boots with every step. In hopes of avoiding any flooding hazards that might crop up, I took time to stop, look around and see exactly how everything was unfolding.

Amazing things happen when you look up.

So many times before, on any number of trips to the Wichitas, the range had revealed itself to be a beautiful, unique place. But it had never looked like this. Sheets of rain obscured the more distant peaks, but the ones closer by had taken an entirely different countenance of slate and silver, the outline of the ridges unified in one long, jagged edge across the horizon, a deeper shade of gray than the rain falling from the clouds above. Those cooler, misty colors are what prompted thoughts of Nordic scenes, and hearing little else besides the rain and the thunder is what made it feel like the range was speaking to me.

Telling me to stop. Telling me to listen and remember what was happening.

So I stopped, listened, and observed.

Right then, no one was seeing what I saw. No one was hearing the rain pound the mountains or thunder echo off the canyon walls. No one in their right mind was out there. I'm sure they'd long since bagged it, heading for their cars or the shelter of some nearby gas station or restaurant. This moment, this intense, magical slice of time, was mine. As much as I would have loved to have shared it with someone, there was no one who would be willing to be there with me. The things I'm telling you now barely give insight. All I can tell you is I felt blessed to be there. These images, sounds and smells are burned into my memory for as long as God will allow me to breathe.

Some people might wonder why I'd go out there alone, and what I just described is your answer. The experiences, and I do mean all of them, are so much more vivid when everything is on you. That buffalo encounter? Yeah, I won't be forgetting that anytime soon. The quiet, spiritual respite at Crab Eyes begs me to go back. Seeing the range swathed in rain was like looking at a new bride, unveiling herself in her wedding dress for the first time for everyone to see.

In the end, I retraced my steps through the thickets and back to the locale of my buffalo encounter, taking care to make lots of noise so whatever was there knew I was coming. I was soaked, tired, hungry and happy. I can remember when I first wrote about it, summing it up thusly:

"It was at that time I realized how lucky I was. At that moment, legions of people were at work. Others were at home watching TV. Some were in jail. Or overseas at war. I was out here, reveling in what was, for me, a unique experience."

Seeing such a surreal scene in a natural setting, something so beautiful, is a little like a drug, a hit taking you somewhere strange and new, and when you come back down the urge to find that spot again is strong. I think that is why I felt so strongly that the wilderness was reminding me of times past when I explored wild places, how profoundly they moved me, and how in the future I'd need to redevelop that sense of wonder, challenge and hardship just to get through the difficulties to come.

And they did come, sharp and stinging in their arrival, and glacially persistent in their duration. When it became too much to bear, I retreated outside, in wild places, and remembered that torrential downpour in those ancient peaks, where I'd narrowly missed a collision with a buffalo, dodged squalls and found myself hopelessly and joyfully engulfed in everything the wilderness could throw at me that day. I guess I could have drank away my pain or found escape at the point of a needle, but the slow death of alcoholism doesn't have a lot of appeal, and quite frankly, hard drugs scare the shit out of me. I have developed a bit of an addiction to the outdoors which can usually be tamed by a good, hard trail run or a day hike in my home stomping grounds.

But that doesn't always last, and from time to time I have to get away. The compulsion is something I'm happy to have, as it's taken me to some incredible places – high summits and their expansive views; lush, wooded valleys and the creatures that live therein – and in so doing, befriend amazing people who have that same call of the wild running through their veins. There are times, particularly after a long, difficult climb, that I swear I'm going to cool it with this outdoorsy stuff, but within minutes of getting back to the trailhead, I'm quietly scheming on how the next outing will unfold. I don't foresee getting this monkey off my back anytime soon.

I think I know why, too. A lot of it has to do with the fact that once the fun is over, and the post-trip crash/letdown has passed, I am left with a pleasant residue of gratitude for what the wilderness has given me. Not too long ago, I took a little time to go on a solo winter camping trip far into the western reaches of the Oklahoma Panhandle. There is a lonely, rugged place out there called Black Mesa, best known as the state's highest point, but in my opinion, worth visiting regardless of its altitude status. It's a locale that suits me – remote, quiet and wild. During the middle of the week on a winter day, you're not going to see anyone there. That was my hope, anyway.

Wish granted. I camped alone at a state park several miles away, rolled up to the trailhead parking lot and saw…. no one. For the better part of the next several hours, it would be me and whatever creatures lived there.

There were three moments from that day that stuck out. The first came when I walked up to the high spot, marked by a stone obelisk showing that I was 4,973 feet above sea level, not all that high compared to a lot of places I'd been, but higher than anywhere else in the state. I looked around and saw little besides the scrub and yucca that managed to crack the dark, volcanic rock forming the mesa.

But as I peered west, I noticed something – it was either a distant cloud bank, all white and misty, or it was a far-off, snowcapped peak. I couldn't tell which. So instead of calling it a day at the summit marker, I walked a little farther west to get a better look.

Eventually I reached the edge of a cliff overlooking a valley that was presumably in New Mexico. And indeed, that white formation was a mountain, graced with snow, ruling over the high plains below. I chose that spot to dig out some food from my pack and grab a bite. So I pulled out a knife, some sausage, cheese and a few rolls, plopped down and dined.

The sweeping view of the valley below was incredible, but that wasn't what hit me. Instead, it was the silence.

It's so rare to hear total quiet, and yet there it was. The wind was down, and if I sat still, all I heard was nothing. On the hike down, I stopped a couple of times to listen for what I thought might have been wildlife, but again, there it was – pure, untrammeled quiet. Again, so rare and beautiful.

In that moment, I felt peace.

The second moment occurred a couple of hours later when I'd finished the hike. The park superintendent where I'd camped the night before had told me where I could see some dinosaur tracks. They were about a quarter mile up the road from the trailhead, so I figured what the heck. How often do you get to see real dinosaur tracks?

I drove up the road, found the turn, and in the bottom of a creek bed, there they were – a line of holes in the rock, some partially filled with water, showing where some really big animal once walked. Pretty cool stuff.

Satisfied I'd made a good day of it, I went back to the car, grabbed some more food and popped open a beer. The menu was the same – sausage, cheese, bread, and an orange. But all that, with the beer, was particularly satisfying after an eight-mile hike. Not exactly Michelin-starred stuff, but I'd be hard-pressed to recall a meal I enjoyed more than that one.

In that moment, I felt content.

The third moment came on the way back, where I made one more stop: A barbecue joint in the small town of Woodward called Wagg's, a place I'd visited years before when I was out there to write about caving at Alabaster Caverns. The food was good, I recalled, so a repeat visit seemed appropriate.

I sat down and placed an order. There were a few other people there, too, gnawing on ribs and jawing about the day's events. A guy on a barstool strummed quiet notes on a guitar while gently crooning country tunes in front of a tip jar. It was completely mellow, almost warm, like the glow and crackle of a fire that calms the spirit while a winter storm rages outside.

I sat there awhile, listening to the music and enjoying my dinner while thinking about what the last two days had given me.

I heard the "sound" of total silence. Roamed an ancient land while having the entire place to myself. Walked in the footsteps of prehistoric behemoths long since gone.

At that moment, I felt gratitude.

I was grateful to have the time and the health to be there. It's rare to have any of these moments, not to mention having them all at once. When you come across such a confluence, you have to acknowledge it. In many ways, it felt so distant from that solo hike through the Wichitas in a driving storm, and yet, inextricably linked as a leg of an ongoing adventure that had taken me to many places between where I was then and where I am now.

Reflecting on that, it makes me wonder: What if you walked into the wilderness and found that you liked it? That in the process of entering that dark, mysterious land you finally came home?

Would it be OK if a concrete destination, a Promised Land, ceased to be the goal and instead your land of milk and honey encompassed the places and people you came to know along the way?

"Settled" doesn't work for some people. When the world of everyday expectations explodes, they simply find a retreat into the wild more comforting, interesting and fulfilling, whether that be in a real wilderness or something more figurative.

I'd say the answer to my question, that of finding home journeying in the wild, is yes. Maybe some of us were meant for wilderness, or wired to wander. It may not be safe, and there can be suffering along the way, just as there was suffering that drove you into the wild in the first place. Strangely, I'm a little grateful for the pain. From where I stand, I wasn't lost, then found. I became found only after I got lost.

PROTECT OUR PUBLIC LANDS

Learn more about Tulsa's Turkey Mountain Urban Wilderness at turkeymtn.com or how to support local conservation efforts there at tulsaurbanwildernesscoalition.org.

To learn more about the Colorado 14ers and how to support conservation efforts in Colorado's high country, go to the Colorado Fourteeners Initiative website at 14ers.org.

ACKNOWLEDGMENTS

No story happens in a vacuum, certainly not mine. Plenty of people have been with me along the way creating these stories.

First off, a huge thanks to my brother Mike. He fueled a lot of my ambitions and gave me a great example to follow not only in the outdoors, but in life. You're missed, big fella.

To the rest of my family – Mom, Dad, Shiela, Steve and Becca – you all have put up with a lot of my wanderlust and risk-taking, but remained encouraging. In this case, enablers are good.

A lot of fun has been had with my Oklahoma posse: Trent, Rick and Jeff. Thanks for coming along on these far-flung trips out West. And Johnny, who helped me get to know the Wichita Mountains while also humoring me on a few Rocky Mountain adventures. All of you have proven to be game for anything while also being great teachers.

My Colorado crew has been indispensable, pushing me to try new things in new places while also giving me valuable perspectives. Bill, Beth, Noel, David and Chuck – thanks for letting this slow flatlander tag along. There are tons of other Colorado folks who have also been on these adventures, and to all of you, let's go climb something again soon. You know who you are.

My life grew richer getting to know people in Tulsa's trail running community. Ken (aka "Trail Zombie," or "TZ" for short) has been the ultimate guide on local trails and embodies the spirit of trail and ultra runners everywhere. And I'd be remiss if I didn't mention Matt, the guy who is everyone's friend, is forever curious and is up for new challenges. I hope to get out to California and see what new trouble we can stir up.

I needed fresh eyes to read this, and I found that in a fellow flatlander and trail hound from Kansas City. Much gratitude to Craig for his editor's eyes while reading through this. Longs Peak still awaits.

It's safe to say this project wouldn't have gone anywhere without Sharryn's editing expertise and publishing guidance. I'm grateful to know you.

Lastly, thanks to God for giving me breath when I wake up, and life as the days have gone by. Going forward, my hope is to make the most of all of them. They're a gift.

Made in the USA
Lexington, KY
16 July 2018